Celebrating the Year of Matthew

28 November 2010 – 26 November 2011

'Prepare the way of the Lord'

VERITAS

The **Gospel** According to

Matthew

(1:1–28:20)

Published 2010 by
Veritas Publications
7–8 Lower Abbey Street
Dublin 1, Ireland
publications@veritas.ie
www.veritas.ie

ISBN 978 1 84730 256 4

A catalogue record for this book is available from the British Library.

Designed by Norma Prause-Brewer.
Printed in the Republic of Ireland by Walsh Colour Print, Kerry.

Veritas books are printed on paper made from the wood pulp of managed forests. For every tree felled, at least one tree is planted, thereby renewing natural resources.

IMAGE USAGE
iStockphoto pp. 10, 11, 12, 14, 15, 16, 17, 18, 19, 20, 21, 23, 24, 25, 26, 31, 34, 35, 36, 37, 38, 39, 40, 41, 43, 44, 45, 46, 47, 48/49, 52, 54, 55, 59, 60, 61, 62, 66, 71, 72, 73, 74, 75, 76, 77, 78, 80, 81, 84, 85, 87, 92/93

Mary Evans Picture Library pp. 8, 11, 12, 39, 40, 41, 42, 53, 58, 64, 65, 68, 69, 70, 82, 83, 84, 85, 86, 87, 88, 90, 91

Wikimedia Commons pp. 6, 7, 9, 12, 13, 17, 26, 27, 28/29, 32, 50, 51, 52, 56, 57, 79

Contents

Introduction 7

The Birth of Jesus and the Beginning of His Ministry (1:1–4:17) 9

The Sermon on the Mount and Miracles in Galilee (4:18–9:38) 16

The Apostles and the Teachings of Jesus (10:1–12:50) 32

The Parables of Jesus (13:1–17:27) 42

Further Teachings of Jesus (18:1–20:34) 58

Jesus' Arrival in Jerusalem (21:1–25:46) 64

The Betrayal, Passion and Death of Jesus (26:1–28:20) 77

Lectio divina 92

Index 94

Bartolomé Esteban Murillo · The Holy Family with a Bird · 1650

The **Gospel** According to Matthew (1:1–28:20)

Guido Reni · St Matthew and the Angel · 1600s

Introduction

The Gospel of Matthew is the first book of the New Testament and is an account of the life, ministry, death and resurrection of Jesus Christ.

The Gospel of Matthew was written between AD 70 and 85. Matthew, one of the first twelve Apostles, wrote mainly for a Jewish community, probably in Syria. He was a Jewish tax collector who left his job to join Jesus. His Gospel stresses how Jesus fulfilled Jewish prophecies and he emphasised obedience to and preservation of biblical law.

This Gospel was written in Greek at least twenty years after Mark's Gospel. Matthew's Gospel follows the outline of Mark's, with a separate section of Jesus' stories, which contains many sayings that he attributes to Jesus. Certain details of Jesus' life, of his infancy in particular, are related only in Matthew.

It was a difficult time for converts as they had to try and find a new identity as Christians and so the Gospel was written for a Church in transition. Matthew reminded them that they had hope – their hope was Jesus Christ.

The longest Gospel of the four, it is noted particularly for its rhythmical and poetic prose, making it a popular liturgical choice, and very suitable for public readings.

The **Birth of Jesus** and the Beginning of **His** Ministry (1:1–4:17)

Matthew gives a brief genealogy of **Jesus of Nazareth**. He also tells of his birth, his baptism by John, and the start of his ministry in Galilee.

chapter ONE

The **Genealogy** of **Jesus** the Messiah

An account of the genealogy of Jesus the Messiah,
the son of David, the son of Abraham.

2Abraham was the father of Isaac, and Isaac the
father of Jacob, and Jacob the father of Judah and
his brothers, 3and Judah the father of Perez and
Zerah by Tamar, and Perez the father of Hezron,
and Hezron the father of Aram, 4and Aram the
father of Aminadab, and Aminadab the father of
Nahshon, and Nahshon the father of Salmon,
5and Salmon the father of Boaz by Rahab,
and Boaz the father of Obed by Ruth,
and Obed the father of Jesse, 6and Jesse
the father of King David.

And David was the father of
Solomon by the wife of Uriah,
7and Solomon the father of
Rehoboam, and Rehoboam the
father of Abijah, and Abijah
the father of Asaph, 8and
Asaph the father of Jehoshaphat, and Jehoshaphat
the father of Joram, and Joram the father of
Uzziah, 9and Uzziah the father of Jotham, and
Jotham the father of Ahaz, and Ahaz the father of
Hezekiah, 10and Hezekiah the father of Manasseh,
and Manasseh the father of Amos, and Amos
the father of Josiah, 11and Josiah the father of
Jechoniah and his brothers, at the time of the
deportation to Babylon.

Giovanni Bellini · Madonna · c. 1510

12And after the deportation to Babylon: Jechoniah
was the father of Salathiel, and Salathiel the
father of Zerubbabel, 13and Zerubbabel the father
of Abiud, and Abiud the father of Eliakim, and
Eliakim the father of Azor, 14and Azor the father
of Zadok, and Zadok the father of Achim, and
Achim the father of Eliud, 15and Eliud the father
of Eleazar, and Eleazar the father of Matthan,
and Matthan the father of Jacob, 16and Jacob the
father of Joseph the husband of Mary, of whom
Jesus was born, who is called the Messiah.

17So all the generations from Abraham to David
are fourteen generations; and from David to the
deportation to Babylon, fourteen generations;
and from the deportation to Babylon to the
Messiah, fourteen generations.

‘She will bear a son, and you are
to name him Jesus, for he will
save his people from their sins.’

The **Birth of Jesus** the Messiah

[18]Now the birth of Jesus the Messiah took place
in this way. When his mother Mary had been
engaged to Joseph, but before they lived together,
she was found to be with child from the Holy
Spirit. [19]Her husband Joseph, being a righteous
man and unwilling to expose her to public
disgrace, planned to dismiss her quietly. [20]But just
when he had resolved to do this, an angel of the
Lord appeared to him in a dream and said, 'Joseph,
son of David, do not be afraid to take Mary as
your wife, for the child conceived in her is from
the Holy Spirit. [21]She will bear a son, and you are
to name him Jesus, for he will save his people from
their sins.' [22]All this took place to fulfil what had
been spoken by the Lord through the prophet:
[23]*'Look, the virgin shall conceive and bear a son, and*
they shall name him Emmanuel',
which means, 'God is with us.' [24]When Joseph
awoke from sleep, he did as the angel of the Lord
commanded him; he took her as his wife, [25]but
had no marital relations with her until she had
borne a son; and he named him Jesus.

Joy!

chapter TWO

The **Visit** of the **Wise Men**

In the time of King Herod, after Jesus was born
in Bethlehem of Judea, wise men from the East
came to Jerusalem, [2]asking, 'Where is the child
who has been born king of the Jews? For we
observed his star at its rising, and have come to
pay him homage.' [3]When King Herod heard this,
he was frightened, and all Jerusalem with him;
[4]and calling together all the chief priests and
scribes of the people, he inquired of them where
the Messiah was to be born. [5]They told him, 'In
Bethlehem of Judea; for so it has been written by
the prophet:
[6]"*And you, Bethlehem, in the land of Judah,*
are by no means least among the rulers of Judah;
for from you shall come a ruler
who is to shepherd my people Israel."'

[7]Then Herod secretly
called for the wise men
and learned from them
the exact time when
the star had appeared.
[8]Then he sent them to
Bethlehem, saying, 'Go
and search diligently for
the child; and when you
have found him, bring me word so that I may also
go and pay him homage.' [9]When they had heard
the king, they set out; and there, ahead of them,
went the star that they had seen at its rising, until
it stopped over the place where the child was.
[10]When they saw that the star had stopped, they
were overwhelmed with joy.

Out of Egypt!

Albrecht Dürer · The Seven Sorrows of the Virgin: The Flight into Egypt · c. 1496

11On entering the
house, they saw the
child with Mary his
mother; and they
knelt down and paid
him homage. Then,
opening their treasure-
chests, 12And having
been warned in a
dream not to return to Herod, they left for their
own country by another road.

The **Escape to Egypt**

13Now after they had left, an angel of the Lord
appeared to Joseph in a dream and said, 'Get
up, take the child and his mother, and flee to
Egypt, and remain there until I tell you; for
Herod is about to search for the child, to destroy
him.' 14Then Joseph got up, took the child and
his mother by night, and went to Egypt, 15and
remained there until the death of Herod. This
was to fulfil what had been spoken by the Lord
through the prophet, 'Out of Egypt I have called
my son.'

The **Massacre** of the Infants

16When Herod saw that he had been tricked by
the wise men, he was infuriated, and he sent and
killed all the children in and around Bethlehem
who were two years old or under, according to
the time that he had learned from the wise men.
17Then was fulfilled what had been spoken through
the prophet Jeremiah:
18'A voice was heard in Ramah,
wailing and loud lamentation,
Rachel weeping for her children;
she refused to be consoled, because they
are no more.'

The **Return** from Egypt

19When Herod died, an angel of the Lord suddenly
appeared in a dream to Joseph in Egypt and said,
20'Get up, take the child and his mother, and go to
the land of Israel, for those who were seeking the
child's life are dead.' 21Then Joseph got up, took
the child and his mother, and went to the land of
Israel. 22But when he heard that Archelaus was
ruling over Judea in place of his father Herod, he
was afraid to go there. And after being warned in
a dream, he went away to the district of Galilee.
23There he made his home in a town called
Nazareth, so that what had been spoken through
the prophets might be fulfilled, 'He will be called
a Nazorean.'

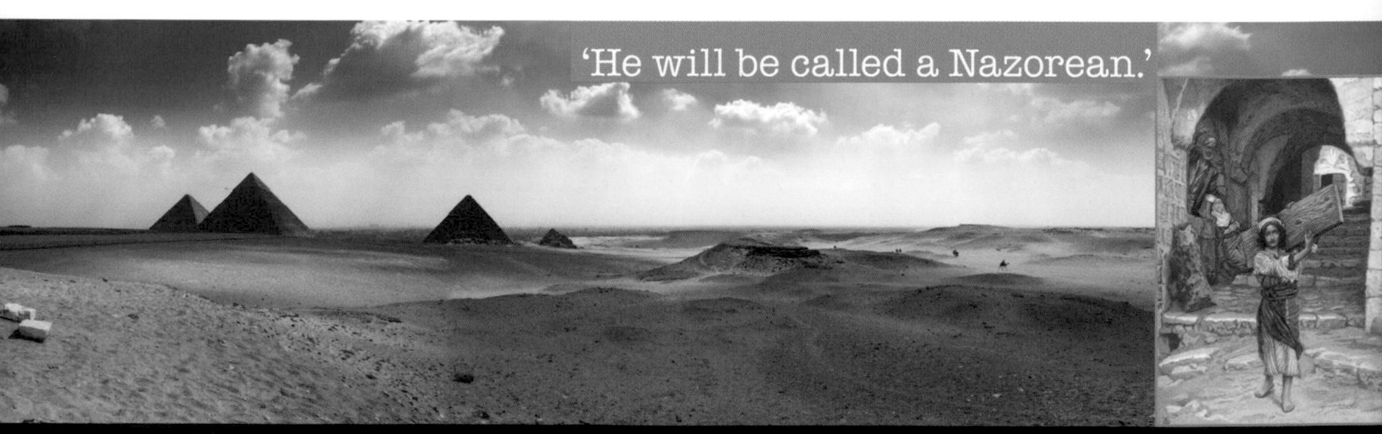
'He will be called a Nazorean.'

rtolomé Esteban Perez Murillo · The Holy Children with a Shell · c. 17th Century

'Prepare the way of the Lord ...'

chapter THREE

The **Proclamation** of **John the Baptist**

In those days John the Baptist appeared in the
wilderness of Judea, proclaiming, 2'Repent, for
the kingdom of heaven has come near.' 3This is the
one of whom the prophet Isaiah spoke when he
said,

'The voice of one crying out in the wilderness:
"Prepare the way of the Lord,
make his paths straight."'

4Now John wore clothing of camel's hair with
a leather belt around his waist, and his food
was locusts and wild honey. 5Then the people
of Jerusalem and all Judea were going out to
him, and all the region along the Jordan, 6and
they were baptised by him in the river Jordan,
confessing their sins.

7But when he saw many Pharisees and Sadducees
coming for baptism, he said to them, 'You brood
of vipers! Who warned you to flee from the wrath
to come? 8Bear fruit worthy of repentance. 9Do
not presume to say to yourselves, "We have
Abraham as our ancestor"; for I tell you, God is
able from these stones to raise up children to
Abraham. 10Even now the axe is lying at the root
of the trees; every tree therefore that does not
bear good fruit is cut down and thrown into the
fire.
11'I baptise you with water for repentance, but one
who is more powerful than I is coming after me; I
am not worthy to carry his sandals. He will baptise
you with the Holy Spirit and fire. 12His winnowing-
fork is in his hand, and he will clear his threshing-
floor and will gather his wheat into the granary;
but the chaff he will burn with unquenchable fire.'

The **Baptism of Jesus**

13Then Jesus came from Galilee to John at the
Jordan, to be baptised by him. 14John would have
prevented him, saying, 'I need to be baptised
by you, and do you come to me?' 15But Jesus
answered him, 'Let it be so now; for it is proper for
us in this way to fulfil all righteousness.' Then he
consented. 16And when Jesus had been baptised,
just as he came up from the water, suddenly the
heavens were opened to him and he saw the Spirit
of God descending like a dove and alighting on
him. 17And a voice from heaven said, 'This is my
Son, the Beloved, with whom I am well pleased.'

chapter FOUR

'Worship the Lord your God, and serve only him.'

The **Temptation** of Jesus

Then Jesus was led up by the Spirit
into the wilderness to be tempted by
the devil. 2He fasted for forty days
and forty nights, and afterwards he
was famished. 3The tempter came
and said to him, 'If you are the Son
of God, command these stones to
become loaves of bread.' 4But he answered, 'It is
written,

"One does not live by bread alone,
but by every word that comes from the mouth of God."'

5Then the devil took him to the holy city and
placed him on the pinnacle of the temple, 6saying
to him, 'If you are the Son of God, throw yourself
down; for it is written,

"He will command his angels concerning you",
and
"On their hands they will bear you up,
so that you will not dash your foot against a stone."'

7Jesus said to him, 'Again it is written,
"Do not put the Lord your God to the test."'

8Again, the devil took him to a very high mountain
and showed him all the kingdoms of the world and
their splendour; 9and he said to him, 'All these I
will give you, if you will fall down and worship me.'
10Jesus said to him, 'Away with you, Satan! for it is
written,

"Worship the Lord your God,
and serve only him."'

11Then the devil left him, and suddenly angels
came and waited on him.

Jesus Begins His **Ministry in Galilee**

12Now when Jesus heard that John had been
arrested, he withdrew to Galilee. 13He left
Nazareth and made his home in Capernaum by
the lake, in the territory of Zebulun and Naphtali,
14so that what had been spoken through the
prophet Isaiah might be fulfilled:

15'Land of Zebulun, land of Naphtali,
on the road by the sea, across the Jordan,
Galilee of the Gentiles –
16the people who sat in darkness
have seen a great light,
and for those who sat in the region and shadow of death
light has dawned.'

17From that time Jesus began to proclaim, 'Repent,
for the kingdom of heaven has come near.

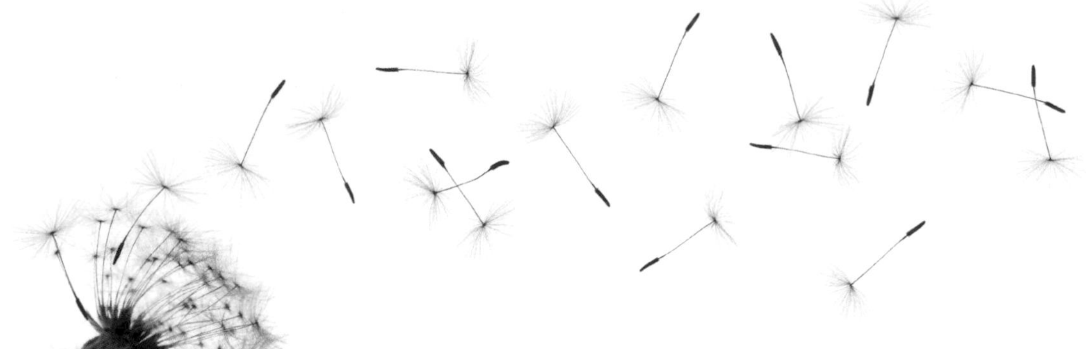

The **Sermon** on the Mount and **Miracles** in **Galilee**

(4:18–9:38)

The **teachings of Jesus**, including the **Beatitudes**.

Jesus Calls the First Disciples

[18]As he walked by the Sea of Galilee, he saw
two brothers, Simon, who is called Peter, and
Andrew his brother, casting a net into the lake
– for they were fishermen. [19]And he said to
them, 'Follow me, and I will make you fish for
people.' [20]Immediately they left their nets and
followed him. [21]As he went from there, he saw
two other brothers, James son of Zebedee and
his brother John, in the boat with their father
Zebedee, mending their nets, and he called them.
[22]Immediately they left the boat and their father,
and followed him.

Jesus Ministers to Crowds of People

[23]Jesus went throughout Galilee, teaching in
their synagogues and proclaiming the good news
of the kingdom and curing every disease and
every sickness among the people. [24]So his fame
spread throughout all Syria, and they brought to
him all the sick, those who were afflicted with
various diseases and pains, demoniacs, epileptics,
and paralytics, and he cured them. [25]And great
crowds followed him from Galilee, the Decapolis,
Jerusalem, Judea, and from beyond the Jordan.

'Follow me, and I will make you fish for people.'

chapter FIVE

The **Beatitudes**

When Jesus saw the crowds, he went up the mountain; and after he sat down, his disciples came to him. 2Then he began to speak, and taught them, saying:

3'Blessed are the poor in spirit, for theirs is the kingdom of heaven.

4'Blessed are those who mourn, for they will be comforted.

5'Blessed are the meek, for they will inherit the earth.

6'Blessed are those who hunger and thirst for righteousness, for they will be filled.

7'Blessed are the merciful, for they will receive mercy.

8'Blessed are the pure in heart, for they will see God.

9'Blessed are the peacemakers, for they will be called children of God.

10'Blessed are those who are persecuted for righteousness' sake, for theirs is the kingdom of heaven.

11'Blessed are you when people revile you and
persecute you and utter all kinds of evil against
you falsely on my account. 12Rejoice and be glad,
for your reward is great in heaven, for in the
same way they persecuted the prophets who
were before you.

Salt and **Light**

13'You are the salt of the earth; but if salt has lost its taste, how can its saltiness be restored? It is no longer good for anything, but is thrown out and trampled under foot.

14'You are the light of the world. A city built on
a hill cannot be hidden. 15No one after lighting a
lamp puts it under the bushel basket, but on the
lampstand, and it gives light to all in the house.
16In the same way, let your light shine before
others, so that they may see your good works and
give glory to your Father in heaven.

Blessed! are you!

The Law and the Prophets

17‘Do not think that I have come to abolish the
law or the prophets; I have come not to abolish
but to fulfil. 18For truly I tell you, until heaven
and earth pass away, not one letter, not one
stroke of a letter, will pass from the law until all
is accomplished. 19Therefore, whoever breaks
one of the least of these commandments, and
teaches others to do the same, will be called least
in the kingdom of heaven; but whoever does
them and teaches them will be called great in the
kingdom of heaven. 20For I tell you, unless your
righteousness exceeds that of the scribes and
Pharisees, you will never enter the kingdom of
heaven.

Concerning **Anger**

21‘You have heard that it was said to those of
ancient times, “You shall not murder”; and
“whoever murders shall be liable to judgement.”
22But I say to you that if you are angry with a
brother or sister, you will be liable to judgement;
and if you insult a brother or sister, you will be
liable to the council; and if you say, “You fool”, you
will be liable to the hell of fire. 23So when you are
offering your gift at the altar, if you remember
that your brother or sister has something against
you, 24leave your gift there before the altar and
go; first be reconciled to your brother or sister,
and then come and offer your gift. 25Come to
terms quickly with your accuser while you are on
the way to court with him, or your accuser may
hand you over to the judge, and the judge to the
guard, and you will be thrown into prison. 26Truly I
tell you, you will never get out until you have paid
the last penny.

Concerning **Adultery**

27‘You have heard that it was said, “You shall not
commit adultery.” 28But I say to you that everyone
who looks at a woman with lust has already
committed adultery with her in his heart. 29If your
right eye causes you to sin, tear it out and throw
it away; it is better for you to lose one of your
members than for your whole body to be thrown
into hell. 30And if your right hand causes you to
sin, cut it off and throw it away; it is better for you
to lose one of your members than for your whole
body to go into hell.

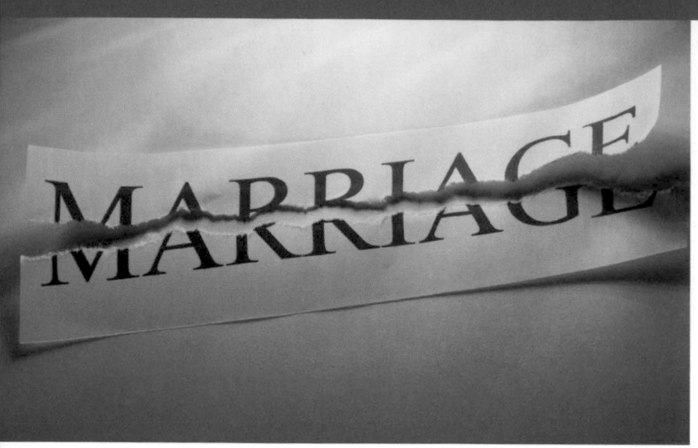

Concerning **Divorce**

31'It was also said, "Whoever divorces his wife, let
him give her a certificate of divorce." 32But I say
to you that anyone who divorces his wife, except
on the ground of unchastity, causes her to commit
adultery; and whoever marries a divorced woman
commits adultery.

Concerning **Oaths**

33'Again, you have heard that it was said to those of ancient times, "You
shall not swear falsely, but carry out the vows you have made to the Lord."
34But I say to you, Do not swear at all, either by heaven, for it is the throne
of God, 35or by the earth, for it is his footstool, or by Jerusalem, for it is the
city of the great King. 36And do not swear by your head, for you cannot
make one hair white or black. 37Let your word be "Yes, Yes" or "No, No";
anything more than this comes from the evil one.

Concerning **Retaliation**

38'You have heard that it was said, "An eye for an
eye and a tooth for a tooth." 39But I say to you, Do
not resist an evildoer. But if anyone strikes you
on the right cheek, turn the other also; 40and if
anyone wants to sue you and take your coat, give
your cloak as well; 41and if anyone forces you to
go one mile, go also the second mile. 42Give to
everyone who begs from you, and do not refuse
anyone who wants to borrow from you.

Love for **Enemies**

43'You have heard that it was said, "You shall love
your neighbour and hate your enemy." 44But I
say to you, Love your enemies and pray for those
who persecute you, 45so that you may be children
of your Father in heaven; for he makes his sun
rise on the evil and on the good, and sends rain
on the righteous and on the unrighteous. 46For
if you love those who love you, what reward do
you have? Do not even the tax-collectors do the
same? 47And if you greet only your brothers and
sisters, what more are you doing than others? Do
not even the Gentiles do the same? 48Be perfect,
therefore, as your heavenly Father is perfect.

chapter **SIX**

Concerning **Almsgiving**

'Beware of practising your piety before others in order to be seen by them; for then you have no reward from your Father in heaven.

2'So whenever you give alms, do not sound a
trumpet before you, as the hypocrites do in the
synagogues and in the streets, so that they may
be praised by others. Truly I tell you, they have
received their reward. 3But when you give alms,
do not let your left hand know what your right
hand is doing, 4so that your alms may be done
in secret; and your Father who sees in secret will
reward you.

Concerning **Prayer**

5'And whenever you pray, do not be like the
hypocrites; for they love to stand and pray in the
synagogues and at the street corners, so that they
may be seen by others. Truly I tell you, they have
received their reward. 6But whenever you pray, go
into your room and shut the door and pray to your
Father who is in secret; and your Father who sees
in secret will reward you.

7'When you are praying, do not heap up empty
phrases as the Gentiles do; for they think that
they will be heard because of their many words.
8Do not be like them, for your Father knows what
you need before you ask him.

9'Pray then in this way:
Our Father in heaven,
hallowed be your name.
10Your kingdom come.
Your will be done,
on earth as it is in heaven.
11Give us this day our daily bread.
12And forgive us our debts,
as we also have forgiven our debtors.
13And do not bring us to the time of trial,
but rescue us from the evil one.
14For if you forgive others their trespasses, your
heavenly Father will also forgive you; 15but if you
do not forgive others, neither will your Father
forgive your trespasses.

'... do not let your left hand know what your right hand is doing ...'

Concerning **Fasting**

16‘And whenever you fast, do not look dismal, like
the hypocrites, for they disfigure their faces so as
to show others that they are fasting. Truly I tell
you, they have received their reward. 17But when
you fast, put oil on your head and wash your face,
18so that your fasting may be seen not by others
but by your Father who is in secret; and your
Father who sees in secret will reward you.

Concerning **Treasures**

19‘Do not store up for yourselves treasures on
earth, where moth and rust consume and where
thieves break in and steal; 20but store up for
yourselves treasures in heaven, where neither
moth nor rust consumes and where thieves do not
break in and steal. 21For where your treasure is,
there your heart will be also.

The **Sound Eye**

22‘The eye is the lamp of the body. So, if your eye
is healthy, your whole body will be full of light;
23but if your eye is unhealthy, your whole body
will be full of darkness. If then the light in you is
darkness, how great is the darkness!

Serving **Two Masters**

24‘No one can serve two masters; for a slave will
either hate the one and love the other, or be
devoted to the one and despise the other. You
cannot serve God and wealth.

Do Not Worry

25‘Therefore I tell you, do not worry about your
life, what you will eat or what you will drink, or
about your body, what you will wear. Is not life
more than food, and the body more than clothing?
26Look at the birds of the air; they neither sow nor
reap nor gather into barns, and yet your heavenly
Father feeds them. Are you not of more value
than they? 27And can any of you by worrying add
a single hour to your span of life? 28And why do
you worry about clothing? Consider the lilies of
the field, how they grow; they neither toil nor
spin, 29yet I tell you, even Solomon in all his glory
was not clothed like one of these. 30But if God
so clothes the grass of the field, which is alive
today and tomorrow is thrown into the oven,
will he not much more clothe you – you of little
faith? 31Therefore do not worry, saying, “What
will we eat?” or “What will we drink?” or “What
will we wear?” 32For it is the Gentiles who strive
for all these things; and indeed your heavenly
Father knows that you need all these things.
33But strive first for the kingdom of God and his
righteousness, and all these things will be given to
you as well.

34‘So do not worry about tomorrow, for tomorrow
will bring worries of its own. Today’s trouble is
enough for today.

‘In everything do to others as you would have them do to you; for this is the law and the prophets.’

chapter **SEVEN**

Judging Others

'Do not judge, so that you may not be judged. 2For
with the judgement you make you will be judged,
and the measure you give will be the measure
you get. 3Why do you see the speck in your
neighbour's eye, but do not notice the log in your
own eye? 4Or how can you say to your neighbour,
"Let me take the speck out of your eye", while the
log is in your own eye? 5You hypocrite, first take
the log out of your own eye, and then you will see
clearly to take the speck out of your neighbour's
eye.

Profaning the Holy

6'Do not give what is holy to dogs; and do not
throw your pearls before swine, or they will
trample them under foot and turn and maul you.

Ask, Search, Knock

7'Ask, and it will be given to you; search, and
you will find; knock, and the door will be opened
for you. 8For everyone who asks receives, and
everyone who searches finds, and for everyone
who knocks, the door will be opened. 9Is there
anyone among you who, if your child asks for
bread, will give a stone? 10Or if the child asks for
a fish, will give a snake? 11If you then, who are evil,
know how to give good gifts to your children, how
much more will your Father in heaven give good
things to those who ask him!

The **Golden Rule**

12'In everything do to others as you would
have them do to you; for this is the law and the
prophets.

The **Narrow Gate**

13'Enter through the narrow gate; for the gate
is wide and the road is easy that leads to
destruction, and there are many who take it. 14For
the gate is narrow and the road is hard that leads
to life, and there are few who find it.

Ask

A **Tree** and Its **Fruit**

15‘Beware of false prophets, who come to you
in sheep’s clothing but inwardly are ravenous
wolves. 16You will know them by their fruits. Are
grapes gathered from thorns, or figs from thistles?
17In the same way, every good tree bears good
fruit, but the bad tree bears bad fruit. 18A good
tree cannot bear bad fruit, nor can a bad tree bear
good fruit. 19Every tree that does not bear good
fruit is cut down and thrown into the fire. 20Thus
you will know them by their fruits.

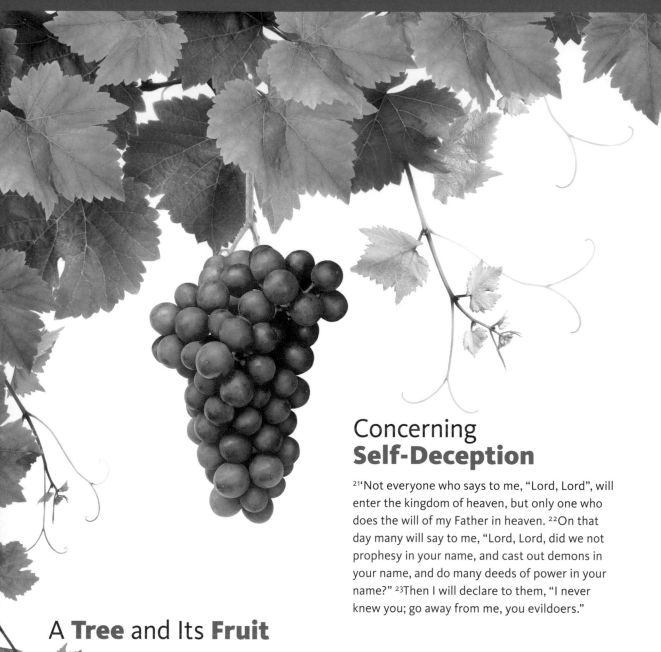

Concerning **Self-Deception**

21‘Not everyone who says to me, “Lord, Lord”, will
enter the kingdom of heaven, but only one who
does the will of my Father in heaven. 22On that
day many will say to me, “Lord, Lord, did we not
prophesy in your name, and cast out demons in
your name, and do many deeds of power in your
name?” 23Then I will declare to them, “I never
knew you; go away from me, you evildoers.”

Hearers and **Doers**

24'Everyone then who hears these words of mine
and acts on them will be like a wise man who built
his house on rock. 25The rain fell, the floods came,
and the winds blew and beat on that house, but it
did not fall, because it had been founded on rock.
26And everyone who hears these words of mine
and does not act on them will be like a foolish
man who built his house on sand. 27The rain fell,
and the floods came, and the winds blew and beat
against that house, and it fell – and great was its
fall!'

28Now when Jesus had finished saying these
things, the crowds were astounded at his
teaching, 29for he taught them as one having
authority, and not as their scribes.

'Everyone then who hears these words of mine and acts on them will be like a wise man who built his house on rock.'

Duccio di Buoninsegna · The Healing of the Blind Man · 1308–1311

chapter EIGHT

Jesus **Cleanses a Leper**

When Jesus had come down from the
mountain, great crowds followed him; 2and
there was a leper who came to him and knelt
before him, saying, 'Lord, if you choose, you
can make me clean.' 3He stretched out his
hand and touched him, saying, 'I do choose.
Be made clean!' Immediately his leprosy was
cleansed. 4Then Jesus said to him, 'See that
you say nothing to anyone; but go, show
yourself to the priest, and offer the gift that
Moses commanded, as a testimony to them.'

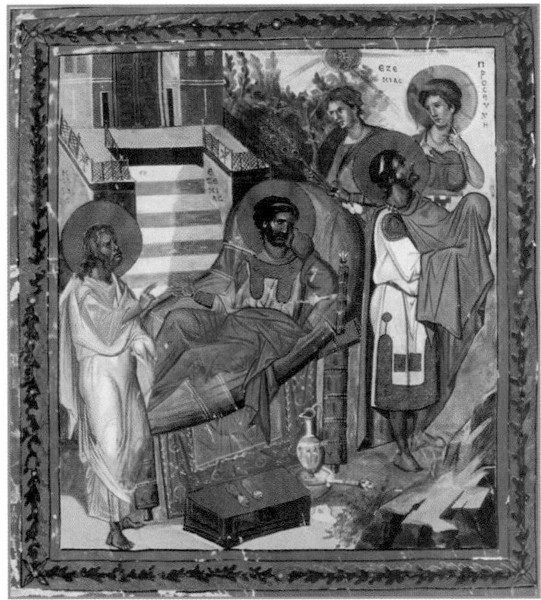

Paris Psalter · Byzantine Illuminated Manuscript · c. 10th century

Jesus Heals a Centurion's Servant

5When he entered Capernaum, a centurion came
to him, appealing to him 6and saying, 'Lord, my
servant is lying at home paralysed, in terrible
distress.' 7And he said to him, 'I will come and
cure him.' 8The centurion answered, 'Lord, I am
not worthy to have you come under my roof;
but only speak the word, and my servant will be
healed. 9For I also am a man under authority, with
soldiers under me; and I say to one, "Go", and
he goes, and to another, "Come", and he comes,
and to my slave, "Do this", and the slave does it.'
10When Jesus heard him, he was amazed and said
to those who followed him, 'Truly I tell you, in no
one in Israel have I found such faith. 11I tell you,
many will come from east and west and will eat
with Abraham and Isaac and Jacob in the kingdom
of heaven, 12while the heirs of the kingdom will
be thrown into the outer darkness, where there
will be weeping and gnashing of teeth.' 13And to
the centurion Jesus said, 'Go; let it be done for
you according to your faith.' And the servant was
healed in that hour.

Jesus Heals Many at **Peter's House**

14When Jesus entered Peter's house, he saw his
mother-in-law lying in bed with a fever; 15he
touched her hand, and the fever left her, and she
got up and began to serve him. 16That evening
they brought to him many who were possessed
by demons; and he cast out the spirits with a
word, and cured all who were sick. 17This was to
fulfil what had been spoken through the prophet
Isaiah, 'He took our infirmities and bore our
diseases.'

Would-Be **Followers of Jesus**

18Now when Jesus saw great crowds around him,
he gave orders to go over to the other side. 19A
scribe then approached and said, 'Teacher, I will
follow you wherever you go.' 20And Jesus said to
him, 'Foxes have holes, and birds of the air have
nests; but the Son of Man has nowhere to lay his
head.' 21Another of his disciples said to him, 'Lord,
first let me go and bury my father.' 22But Jesus
said to him, 'Follow me, and let the dead bury
their own dead.'

Jesus **Stills the Storm**

[23]And when he got into the boat, his disciples
followed him. [24]A gale arose on the lake, so great
that the boat was being swamped by the waves;
but he was asleep. [25]And they went and woke him
up, saying, 'Lord, save us! We are perishing!' [26]And
he said to them, 'Why are you afraid, you of little
faith?' Then he got up and rebuked the winds and
the sea; and there was a dead calm. [27]They were
amazed, saying, 'What sort of man is this, that
even the winds and the sea obey him?'

Jesus Heals the Gadarene Demoniacs

[28]When he came to the other side, to the country
of the Gadarenes, two demoniacs coming out of
the tombs met him. They were so fierce that no
one could pass that way. [29]Suddenly they shouted,
'What have you to do with us, Son of God? Have
you come here to torment us before the time?'
[30]Now a large herd of swine was feeding at some
distance from them. [31]The demons begged him, 'If
you cast us out, send us into the herd of swine.'
[32]And he said to them, 'Go!' So they came out and
entered the swine; and suddenly, the whole herd
rushed down the steep bank into the lake and
perished in the water. [33]The swineherds ran off,
and on going into the town, they told the whole
story about what had happened to the demoniacs.
[34]Then the whole town came out to meet Jesus;
and when they saw him, they begged him to leave
their neighbourhood.

chapter **NINE**

Jesus Heals a Paralytic

And after getting into a boat he crossed the water
and came to his own town. 2And just then some
people were carrying a paralysed man lying on
a bed. When Jesus saw their faith, he said to the
paralytic, 'Take heart, son; your sins are forgiven.'
3Then some of the scribes said to themselves,
'This man is blaspheming.' 4But Jesus, perceiving
their thoughts, said, 'Why do you think evil in
your hearts? 5For which is easier, to say, "Your sins
are forgiven", or to say, "Stand up and walk"? 6'But
so that you may know that the Son of Man has
authority on earth to forgive sins' – he then said
to the paralytic – 'Stand up, take your bed and go
to your home.' 7And he stood up and went to his
home. 8When the crowds saw it, they were filled
with awe, and they glorified God, who had given
such authority to human beings.

Matthew!

The Calling of Matthew

9As Jesus was walking along, he saw a man called
Matthew sitting at the tax booth; and he said to
him, 'Follow me.' And he got up and followed him.
10And as he sat at dinner in the house, many
tax-collectors and sinners came and were sitting
with him and his disciples. 11When the Pharisees
saw this, they said to his disciples, 'Why does
your teacher eat with tax-collectors and sinners?'
12But when he heard this, he said, 'Those who are
well have no need of a physician, but those who
are sick. 13Go and learn what this means, "I desire
mercy, not sacrifice." For I have come to call not
the righteous but sinners.'

Rembrandt van Rijn · The Storm on the Sea of Galilee · 1633

The Question about **Fasting**

14Then the disciples of John came to him, saying,
'Why do we and the Pharisees fast often, but your
disciples do not fast?' 15And Jesus said to them,
'The wedding-guests cannot mourn as long as the
bridegroom is with them, can they? The days will
come when the bridegroom is taken away from
them, and then they will fast. 16No one sews a
piece of unshrunk cloth on an old cloak, for the
patch pulls away from the cloak, and a worse
tear is made. 17Neither is new wine put into old
wineskins; otherwise, the skins burst, and the
wine is spilled, and the skins are destroyed; but
new wine is put into fresh wineskins, and so both
are preserved.'

A Girl Restored to Life and a Woman Healed

18While he was saying these things to them,
suddenly a leader of the synagogue came in and
knelt before him, saying, 'My daughter has just
died; but come and lay your hand on her, and
she will live.' 19And Jesus got up and followed
him, with his disciples. 20Then suddenly a woman
who had been suffering from haemorrhages for
twelve years came up behind him and touched
the fringe of his cloak, 21for she said to herself,
'If I only touch his cloak, I will be made well.'
22Jesus turned, and seeing her he said, 'Take
heart, daughter; your faith has made you well.'
And instantly the woman was made well. 23When
Jesus came to the leader's house and saw the
flute-players and the crowd making a commotion,

24he said, 'Go away; for the girl is not dead but
sleeping.' And they laughed at him. 25But when
the crowd had been put outside, he went in and
took her by the hand, and the girl got up. 26And
the report of this spread throughout that district.

Jesus Heals Two Blind Men

27As Jesus went on from there, two blind men
followed him, crying loudly, 'Have mercy on us,
Son of David!' 28When he entered the house, the
blind men came to him; and Jesus said to them,
'Do you believe that I am able to do this?' They
said to him, 'Yes, Lord.' 29Then he touched their
eyes and said, 'According to your faith let it be
done to you.' 30And their eyes were opened. Then
Jesus sternly ordered them, 'See that no one
knows of this.' 31But they went away and spread
the news about him throughout that district.

Jesus Heals

'Never has anything like this been seen in Israel.'

Rejoice!

Jesus Heals One Who Was Mute

32After they had gone away, a demoniac who was
mute was brought to him. 33And when the demon
had been cast out, the one who had been mute
spoke; and the crowds were amazed and said,
'Never has anything like this been seen in Israel.'
34But the Pharisees said, 'By the ruler of the
demons he casts out the demons.'

The **Harvest is Great**, the Labourers Few

35Then Jesus went about all the cities and villages,
teaching in their synagogues, and proclaiming
the good news of the kingdom, and curing every
disease and every sickness. 36When he saw the
crowds, he had compassion for them, because
they were harassed and helpless, like sheep
without a shepherd. 37Then he said to his disciples,
'The harvest is plentiful, but the labourers are few;
38therefore ask the Lord of the harvest to send out
labourers into his harvest.'

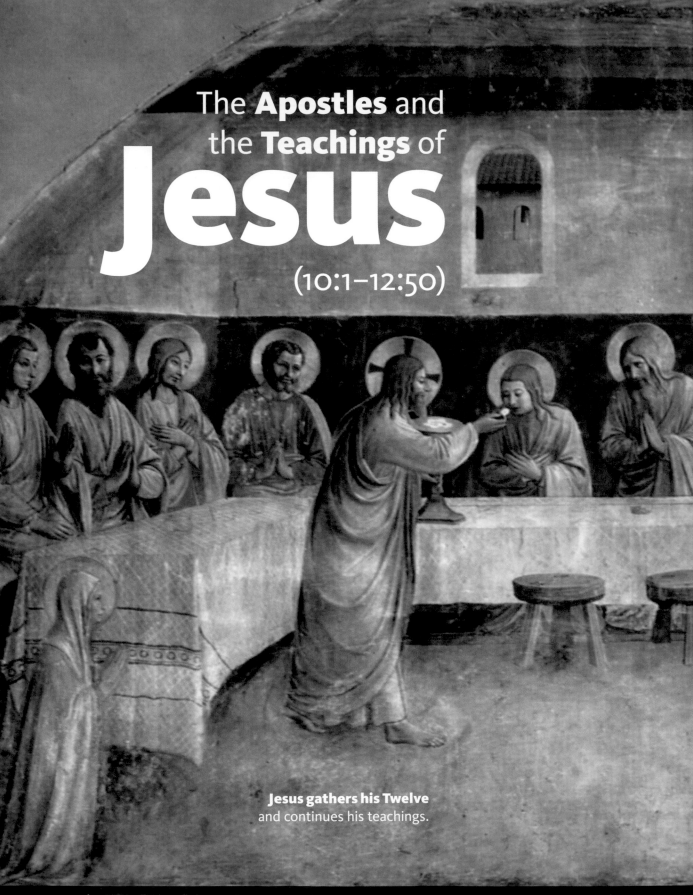

The **Apostles** and the **Teachings** of Jesus (10:1–12:50)

Jesus gathers his Twelve and continues his teachings.

Fra Angelico · Communion of the Apostles · c. 1437–1446

chapter **TEN**

The Twelve Apostles

Then Jesus summoned his twelve disciples and
gave them authority over unclean spirits, to cast
them out, and to cure every disease and every
sickness. 2These are the names of the twelve
apostles: first, Simon, also known as Peter, and his
brother Andrew; James son of Zebedee, and his
brother John; 3Philip and Bartholomew; Thomas
and Matthew the tax-collector; James son of
Alphaeus, and Thaddaeus; 4Simon the Cananaean,
and Judas Iscariot, the one who betrayed him.

The **Mission** of the Twelve

5These twelve Jesus sent out with the following
instructions: 'Go nowhere among the Gentiles,
and enter no town of the Samaritans, 6but go
rather to the lost sheep of the house of Israel. 7As
you go, proclaim the good news, "The kingdom
of heaven has come near." 8Cure the sick, raise
the dead, cleanse the lepers, cast out demons.
You received without payment; give without
payment. 9Take no gold, or silver, or copper in
your belts, 10no bag for your journey, or two
tunics, or sandals, or a staff; for labourers deserve
their food. 11Whatever town or village you enter,
find out who in it is worthy, and stay there until
you leave. 12As you enter the house, greet it. 13If
the house is worthy, let your peace come upon
it; but if it is not worthy, let your peace return to
you. 14If anyone will not welcome you or listen to
your words, shake off the dust from your feet as
you leave that house or town. 15Truly I tell you, it
will be more tolerable for the land of Sodom and
Gomorrah on the day of judgement than for that
town.

‘... the one who endures to the end will be saved.’

Coming **Persecutions**

16‘See, I am sending you out like sheep into the
midst of wolves; so be wise as serpents and
innocent as doves. 17Beware of them, for they
will hand you over to councils and flog you in
their synagogues; 18and you will be dragged
before governors and kings because of me, as
a testimony to them and the Gentiles. 19When
they hand you over, do not worry about how
you are to speak or what you are to say; for what
you are to say will be given to you at that time;
20for it is not you who speak, but the Spirit of
your Father speaking through you. 21Brother will
betray brother to death, and a father his child,
and children will rise against parents and have
them put to death; 22and you will be hated by all
because of my name. But the one who endures to
the end will be saved. 23When they persecute you
in one town, flee to the next; for truly I tell you,
you will not have gone through all the towns of
Israel before the Son of Man comes.
24‘A disciple is not above the teacher, nor a slave
above the master; 25it is enough for the disciple to
be like the teacher, and the slave like the master.
If they have called the master of the house
Beelzebul, how much more will they malign those
of his household!

Whom to **Fear**

26'So have no fear of them; for nothing is covered
up that will not be uncovered, and nothing secret
that will not become known. 27What I say to you
in the dark, tell in the light; and what you hear
whispered, proclaim from the housetops. 28Do not
fear those who kill the body but cannot kill the
soul; rather fear him who can destroy both soul
and body in hell. 29Are not two sparrows sold for a
penny? Yet not one of them will fall to the ground
unperceived by your Father. 30And even the hairs
of your head are all counted. 31So do not be afraid;
you are of more value than many sparrows.

32'Everyone therefore who acknowledges me
before others, I also will acknowledge before
my Father in heaven; 33but whoever denies me
before others, I also will deny before my Father in
heaven.

Not Peace, but a Sword

34'Do not think that I have come to bring peace to
the earth; I have not come to bring peace, but a
sword.
35For I have come to set a man against his father,
and a daughter against her mother,
and a daughter-in-law against her mother-in-law;
36and one's foes will be members of one's own
household.
37Whoever loves father or mother more than me
is not worthy of me; and whoever loves son or
daughter more than me is not worthy of me; 38and
whoever does not take up the cross and follow me
is not worthy of me. 39Those who find their life will
lose it, and those who lose their life for my sake
will find it.

Rewards

40'Whoever welcomes you welcomes me, and
whoever welcomes me welcomes the one who
sent me. 41Whoever welcomes a prophet in the
name of a prophet will receive a prophet's reward;
and whoever welcomes a righteous person in
the name of a righteous person will receive the
reward of the righteous; 42and whoever gives
even a cup of cold water to one of these little ones
in the name of a disciple – truly I tell you, none of
these will lose their reward.'

Proclaim from the housetops!

chapter ELEVEN

Now when Jesus had finished instructing his
twelve disciples, he went on from there to teach
and proclaim his message in their cities.

Messengers from John the Baptist

2When John heard in prison what the Messiah was
doing, he sent word by his disciples 3and said to
him, 'Are you the one who is to come, or are we to
wait for another?' 4Jesus answered them, 'Go and
tell John what you hear and see: 5the blind receive
their sight, the lame walk, the lepers are cleansed,
the deaf hear, the dead are raised, and the poor
have good news brought to them. 6And blessed is
anyone who takes no offence at me.'

Jesus Praises John the Baptist

7As they went away, Jesus began to speak to the
crowds about John: 'What did you go out into
the wilderness to look at? A reed shaken by the
wind? 8What then did you go out to see? Someone
dressed in soft robes? Look, those who wear soft
robes are in royal palaces. 9What then did you go
out to see? A prophet? Yes, I tell you, and more
than a prophet. 10This is the one about whom it is
written,
"*See, I am sending my messenger ahead of you,*
who will prepare your way before you."
11Truly I tell you, among those born of women no
one has arisen greater than John the Baptist; yet
the least in the kingdom of heaven is greater than
he. 12From the days of John the Baptist until now
the kingdom of heaven has suffered violence, and
the violent take it by force. 13For all the prophets
and the law prophesied until John came; 14and if
you are willing to accept it, he is Elijah who is to
come. 15Let anyone with ears listen!

16'But to what will I compare this generation? It
is like children sitting in the market-places and
calling to one another,
17"We played the flute for you, and you did not
dance;
we wailed, and you did not mourn."
18For John came neither eating nor drinking, and
they say, "He has a demon"; 19the Son of Man
came eating and drinking, and they say, "Look, a
glutton and a drunkard, a friend of tax-collectors
and sinners!" Yet wisdom is vindicated by her
deeds.'

'Let anyone with ears listen!'

Woes to Unrepentant Cities

[20]Then he began to reproach the cities in which
most of his deeds of power had been done,
because they did not repent. [21]'Woe to you,
Chorazin! Woe to you, Bethsaida! For if the deeds
of power done in you had been done in Tyre and
Sidon, they would have repented long ago in
sackcloth and ashes. [22]But I tell you, on the day of
judgement it will be more tolerable for Tyre and
Sidon than for you. [23]And you, Capernaum,
will you be exalted to heaven?
No, you will be brought down to Hades.
For if the deeds of power done in you had been
done in Sodom, it would have remained until this
day. [24]But I tell you that on the day of judgement
it will be more tolerable for the land of Sodom
than for you.'

Jesus Thanks His Father

[25]At that time Jesus said, 'I thank you, Father, Lord
of heaven and earth, because you have hidden
these things from the wise and the intelligent
and have revealed them to infants; [26]yes, Father,
for such was your gracious will. [27]All things have
been handed over to me by my Father; and no
one knows the Son except the Father, and no one
knows the Father except the Son and anyone to
whom the Son chooses to reveal him.

[28]'Come to me, all you that are weary and are
carrying heavy burdens, and I will give you rest.
[29]Take my yoke upon you, and learn from me; for
I am gentle and humble in heart, and you will find
rest for your souls. [30]For my yoke is easy, and my
burden is light.'

chapter **TWELVE**

Plucking Grain on the Sabbath

At that time Jesus went through the cornfields on
the sabbath; his disciples were hungry, and they
began to pluck heads of grain and to eat. [2]When
the Pharisees saw it, they said to him, 'Look, your
disciples are doing what is not lawful to do on
the sabbath.' [3]He said to them, 'Have you not
read what David did when he and his companions
were hungry? [4]He entered the house of God and
ate the bread of the Presence, which it was not
lawful for him or his companions to eat, but only
for the priests. [5]Or have you not read in the law
that on the sabbath the priests in the temple
break the sabbath and yet are guiltless? [6]I tell you,
something greater than the temple is here. [7]But if
you had known what this means, "I desire mercy
and not sacrifice", you would not have condemned
the guiltless. [8]For the Son of Man is lord of the
sabbath.'

The Man with the **Withered Hand**

[9]He left that place and entered their synagogue;
[10]a man was there with a withered hand, and they
asked him, 'Is it lawful to cure on the sabbath?'
so that they might accuse him. [11]He said to them,
'Suppose one of you has only one sheep and it
falls into a pit on the sabbath; will you not lay hold
of it and lift it out? [12]How much more valuable is
a human being than a sheep! So it is lawful to do
good on the sabbath.' [13]Then he said to the man,
'Stretch out your hand.' He stretched it out, and
it was restored, as sound as the other. [14]But the
Pharisees went out and conspired against him,
how to destroy him.

God's Chosen Servant

[15]When Jesus became aware of this, he departed.
Many crowds followed him, and he cured all of
them, [16]and he ordered them not to make him
known. [17]This was to fulfil what had been spoken
through the prophet Isaiah:
[18]'Here is my servant, whom I have chosen,
my beloved, with whom my soul is well pleased.
I will put my Spirit upon him,
and he will proclaim justice to the Gentiles.
[19]He will not wrangle or cry aloud,
nor will anyone hear his voice in the streets.
[20]He will not break a bruised reed
or quench a smouldering wick
until he brings justice to victory.
[21]And in his name the Gentiles will hope.'

Jesus and Beelzebul

22Then they brought to him a demoniac who was blind and mute; and he cured him, so that the one who had been mute could speak and see. 23All the crowds were amazed and said, 'Can this be the Son of David?' 24But when the Pharisees heard it, they said, 'It is only by Beelzebul, the ruler of the demons, that this fellow casts out the demons.' 25He knew what they were thinking and said to them, 'Every kingdom divided against itself is laid waste, and no city or house divided against itself will stand. 26If Satan casts out Satan, he is divided against himself; how then will his kingdom stand? 27If I cast out demons by Beelzebul, by whom do your own exorcists cast them out? Therefore they will be your judges. 28But if it is by the Spirit of God that I cast out demons, then the kingdom of God has come to you. 29Or how can one enter a strong man's house and plunder his property, without first tying up the strong man? Then indeed the house can be plundered. 30Whoever is not with me is against me, and whoever does not gather with me scatters. 31Therefore I tell you, people will be forgiven for every sin and blasphemy, but blasphemy against the Spirit will not be forgiven. 32Whoever speaks a word against the Son of Man will be forgiven, but whoever speaks against the Holy Spirit will not be forgiven, either in this age or in the age to come.

A **Tree** and Its **Fruit**

33'Either make the tree good, and its fruit good; or make the tree bad, and its fruit bad; for the tree is known by its fruit. 34You brood of vipers! How can you speak good things, when you are evil? For out of the abundance of the heart the mouth speaks. 35The good person brings good things out of a good treasure, and the evil person brings evil things out of an evil treasure. 36I tell you, on the day of judgement you will have to give an account for every careless word you utter; 37for by your words you will be justified, and by your words you will be condemned.'

'... the kingdom of God has come to you.'

The Sign of **Jonah**

[38]Then some of the scribes and Pharisees said to
him, 'Teacher, we wish to see a sign from you.'
[39]But he answered them, 'An evil and adulterous
generation asks for a sign, but no sign will be
given to it except the sign of the prophet Jonah.
[40]For just as Jonah was for three days and three
nights in the belly of the sea monster, so for three
days and three nights the Son of Man will be in
the heart of the earth. [41]The people of Nineveh
will rise up at the judgement with this generation
and condemn it, because they repented at the
proclamation of Jonah, and see, something
greater than Jonah is here! [42]The queen of the
South will rise up at the judgement with this
generation and condemn it, because she came
from the ends of the earth to listen to the wisdom
of Solomon, and see, something greater than
Solomon is here!

The Return of the **Unclean Spirit**

[43]'When the unclean spirit has gone out of a
person, it wanders through waterless regions
looking for a resting-place, but it finds none.
[44]Then it says, "I will return to my house from
which I came." When it comes, it finds it empty,
swept, and put in order. [45]Then it goes and brings
along seven other spirits more evil than itself, and
they enter and live there; and the last state of that
person is worse than the first. So will it be also
with this evil generation.'

' … so for three days and three nights the Son of Man will be in the heart of the earth.'

The **True Kindred** of Jesus

46While he was still speaking to the crowds, his
mother and his brothers were standing outside,
wanting to speak to him. 47Someone told him,
'Look, your mother and your brothers are
standing outside, wanting to speak to you.' 48But
to the one who had told him this, Jesus replied,
'Who is my mother, and who are my brothers?'
49And pointing to his disciples, he said, 'Here are
my mother and my brothers! 50For whoever
does the will of my Father in heaven is my
brother and sister and mother.'

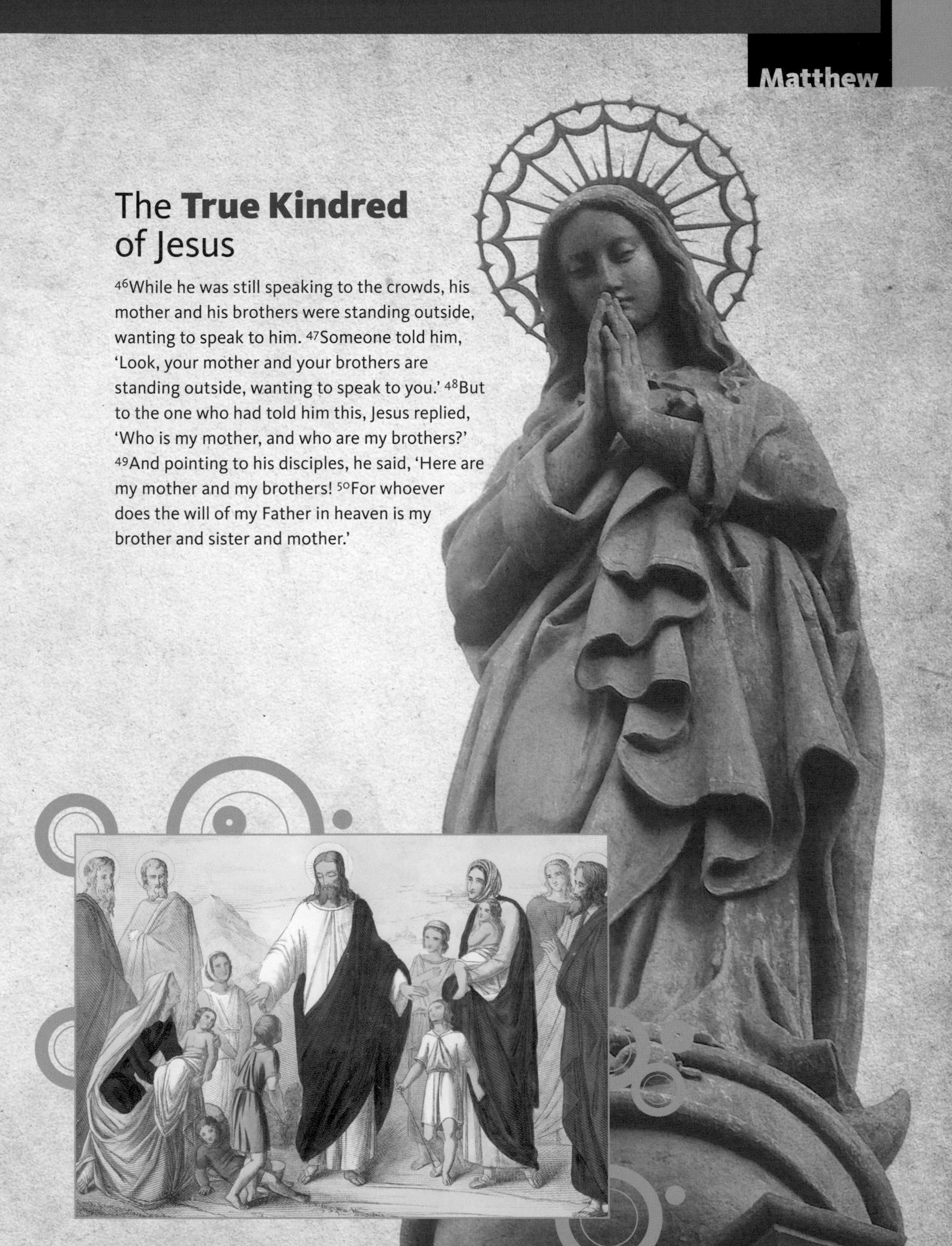

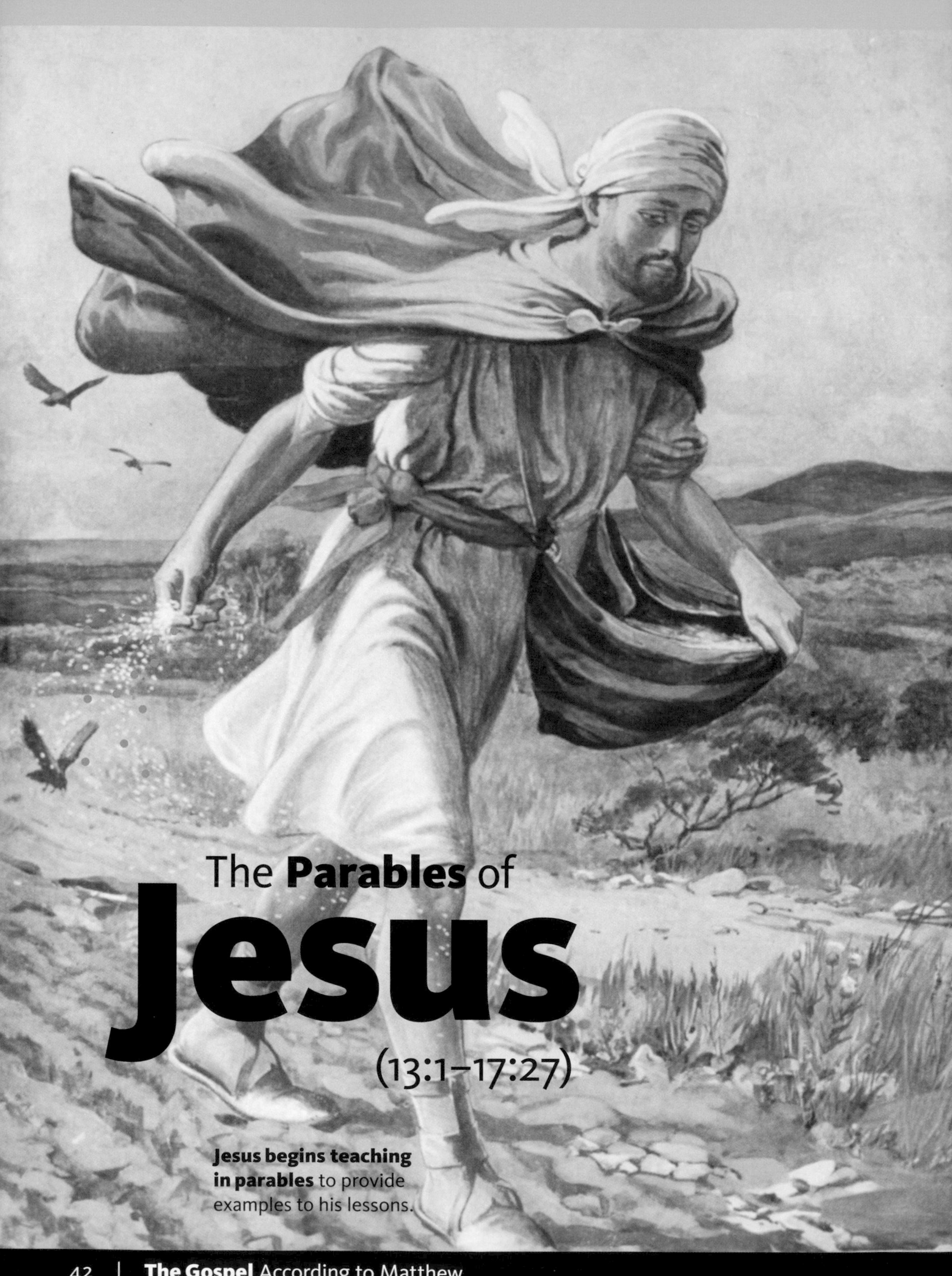

The **Parables** of Jesus

(13:1–17:27)

Jesus begins teaching in parables to provide examples to his lessons.

chapter THIRTEEN

The Parable of the Sower

That same day Jesus went out of the house and
sat beside the lake. 2Such great crowds gathered
around him that he got into a boat and sat there,
while the whole crowd stood on the beach. 3And
he told them many things in parables, saying:
'Listen! A sower went out to sow. 4And as he
sowed, some seeds fell on the path, and the birds
came and ate them up. 5Other seeds fell on rocky
ground, where they did not have much soil, and
they sprang up quickly, since they had no depth of
soil. 6But when the sun rose, they were scorched;
and since they had no root, they withered away.
7Other seeds fell among thorns, and the thorns
grew up and choked them. 8Other seeds fell
on good soil and brought forth grain, some a
hundredfold, some sixty, some thirty. 9Let anyone
with ears listen!'

The Purpose of the Parables

10Then the disciples came and asked him, 'Why do
you speak to them in parables?' 11He answered,
'To you it has been given to know the secrets of
the kingdom of heaven, but to them it has not
been given. 12For to those who have, more will be
given, and they will have an abundance; but from
those who have nothing, even what they have
will be taken away. 13The reason I speak to them
in parables is that "seeing they do not perceive,
and hearing they do not listen, nor do they
understand." 14With them indeed is fulfilled the
prophecy of Isaiah that says:
"You will indeed listen, but never understand,
and you will indeed look, but never perceive.
15For this people's heart has grown dull,
and their ears are hard of hearing,
and they have shut their eyes;
so that they might not look with their eyes,
and listen with their ears,
and understand with their heart and turn –
and I would heal them."
16But blessed are your eyes, for they see, and
your ears, for they hear. 17Truly I tell you, many
prophets and righteous people longed to see what
you see, but did not see it, and to hear what you
hear, but did not hear it.

The Parable of the Sower Explained

18'Hear then the parable of the sower. 19When
anyone hears the word of the kingdom and
does not understand it, the evil one comes and
snatches away what is sown in the heart; this is
what was sown on the path. 20As for what was
sown on rocky ground, this is the one who hears
the word and immediately receives it with joy;
21yet such a person has no root, but endures only
for a while, and when trouble or persecution
arises on account of the word, that person
immediately falls away. 22As for what was sown
among thorns, this is the one who hears the word,
but the cares of the world and the lure of wealth
choke the word, and it yields nothing. 23But as for
what was sown on good soil, this is the one who
hears the word and understands it, who indeed
bears fruit and yields, in one case a hundredfold,
in another sixty, and in another thirty.'

The Parable of Weeds among the Wheat

24He put before them another parable: 'The
kingdom of heaven may be compared to someone
who sowed good seed in his field; 25but while
everybody was asleep, an enemy came and
sowed weeds among the wheat, and then went
away. 26So when the plants came up and bore
grain, then the weeds appeared as well. 27And
the slaves of the householder came and said to
him, "Master, did you not sow good seed in your
field? Where, then, did these weeds come from?"
28He answered, "An enemy has done this." The
slaves said to him, "Then do you want us to go
and gather them?" 29But he replied, "No; for
in gathering the weeds you would uproot the
wheat along with them. 30Let both of them grow
together until the harvest; and at harvest time I
will tell the reapers, Collect the weeds first and
bind them in bundles to be burned, but gather the
wheat into my barn."'

The Parable of the **Mustard Seed**

[31]He put before them another parable: 'The
kingdom of heaven is like a mustard seed that
someone took and sowed in his field; [32]it is the
smallest of all the seeds, but when it has grown it
is the greatest of shrubs and becomes a tree, so
that the birds of the air come and make nests in
its branches.'

The Parable of the **Yeast**

[33]He told them another parable: 'The kingdom of
heaven is like yeast that a woman took and mixed
in with three measures of flour until all of it was
leavened.'

The **Use of Parables**

[34]Jesus told the crowds all these things in
parables; without a parable he told them nothing.
[35]This was to fulfil what had been spoken through
the prophet:
'I will open my mouth to speak in parables;
I will proclaim what has been hidden from the
foundation of the world.'

Jesus Explains the Parable of the Weeds

[36]Then he left the crowds and went into the
house. And his disciples approached him, saying,
'Explain to us the parable of the weeds of the
field.' [37]He answered, 'The one who sows the
good seed is the Son of Man; [38]the field is the
world, and the good seed are the children of
the kingdom; the weeds are the children of the
evil one, [39]and the enemy who sowed them is
the devil; the harvest is the end of the age, and
the reapers are angels. [40]Just as the weeds are
collected and burned up with fire, so will it be at
the end of the age. [41]The Son of Man will send his
angels, and they will collect out of his kingdom
all causes of sin and all evildoers, [42]and they will
throw them into the furnace of fire, where there
will be weeping and gnashing of teeth. [43]Then the
righteous will shine like the sun in the kingdom of
their Father. Let anyone with ears listen!

Three Parables

44‘The kingdom of heaven is like treasure hidden
in a field, which someone found and hid; then in
his joy he goes and sells all that he has and buys
that field.
45‘Again, the kingdom of heaven is like a merchant
in search of fine pearls; 46on finding one pearl of
great value, he went and sold all that he had and
bought it.
47‘Again, the kingdom of heaven is like a net that
was thrown into the sea and caught fish of every
kind; 48when it was full, they drew it ashore, sat
down, and put the good into baskets but threw
out the bad. 49So it will be at the end of the age.
The angels will come out and separate the evil
from the righteous 50and throw them into the
furnace of fire, where there will be weeping and
gnashing of teeth.

Treasures New and Old

51‘Have you understood all this?’ They answered,
‘Yes.’ 52And he said to them, ‘Therefore every
scribe who has been trained for the kingdom of
heaven is like the master of a household who
brings out of his treasure what is new and what is
old.’ 53When Jesus had finished these parables, he
left that place.

The **Rejection** of Jesus at Nazareth

54He came to his home town and began to teach
the people in their synagogue, so that they were
astounded and said, 'Where did this man get
this wisdom and these deeds of power? 55Is not
this the carpenter's son? Is not his mother called
Mary? And are not his brothers James and Joseph
and Simon and Judas? 56And are not all his sisters
with us? Where then did this man get all this?'
57And they took offence at him. But Jesus said to
them, 'Prophets are not without honour except in
their own country and in their own house.' 58And
he did not do many deeds of power there, because
of their unbelief.

'Where did this man get this wisdom and these deeds of power?'

5,000!

chapter FOURTEEN

The Death of John the Baptist

At that time Herod the ruler heard reports about
Jesus; 2and he said to his servants, 'This is John the
Baptist; he has been raised from the dead, and for
this reason these powers are at work in him.' 3For
Herod had arrested John, bound him, and put him in
prison on account of Herodias, his brother Philip's
wife, 4because John had been telling him, 'It is not
lawful for you to have her.' 5Though Herod wanted
to put him to death, he feared the crowd, because
they regarded him as a prophet. 6But when Herod's
birthday came, the daughter of Herodias danced
before the company, and she pleased Herod
7so much that he promised on oath to grant her
whatever she might ask. 8Prompted by her mother,
she said, 'Give me the head of John the Baptist
here on a platter.' 9The king was grieved, yet out
of regard for his oaths and for the guests, he
commanded it to be given; 10he sent and had John
beheaded in the prison. 11The head was brought on
a platter and given to the girl, who brought it to her
mother. 12His disciples came and took the body and
buried it; then they went and told Jesus.

Feeding the Five Thousand

13Now when Jesus heard this, he withdrew from
there in a boat to a deserted place by himself. But
when the crowds heard it, they followed him on
foot from the towns. 14When he went ashore, he
saw a great crowd; and he had compassion for
them and cured their sick. 15When it was evening,
the disciples came to him and said, 'This is a
deserted place, and the hour is now late; send the
crowds away so that they may go into the villages
and buy food for themselves.' 16Jesus said to them,

'They need not go away; you give them something
to eat.' 17They replied, 'We have nothing here but
five loaves and two fish.' 18And he said, 'Bring them
here to me.' 19Then he ordered the crowds to sit
down on the grass. Taking the five loaves and the
two fish, he looked up to heaven, and blessed and
broke the loaves, and gave them to the disciples,
and the disciples gave them to the crowds. 20And
all ate and were filled; and they took up what was
left over of the broken pieces, twelve baskets full.
21And those who ate were about five thousand
men, besides women and children.

Jesus Walks on Water

22Immediately he made the disciples get into the
boat and go on ahead to the other side, while
he dismissed the crowds. 23And after he had
dismissed the crowds, he went up the mountain
by himself to pray. When evening came, he was
there alone, 24but by this time the boat, battered
by the waves, was far from the land, for the wind
was against them. 25And early in the morning he
came walking towards them on the lake. 26But
when the disciples saw him walking on the lake,
they were terrified, saying, 'It is a ghost!' And they
cried out in fear. 27But immediately Jesus spoke to
them and said, 'Take heart, it is I; do not be afraid.'

28Peter answered him, 'Lord, if it is you, command
me to come to you on the water.' 29He said,
'Come.' So Peter got out of the boat, started
walking on the water, and came towards Jesus.
30But when he noticed the strong wind, he
became frightened, and beginning to sink, he
cried out, 'Lord, save me!' 31Jesus immediately
reached out his hand and caught him, saying
to him, 'You of little faith, why did you doubt?'
32When they got into the boat, the wind ceased.
33And those in the boat worshipped him, saying,
'Truly you are the Son of God.'

Lluís Borrassà · St Peter is Walking on the Water · 1411–1413

Jesus **Heals the Sick** in Gennesaret

34When they had crossed over, they came to land
at Gennesaret. 35After the people of that place
Recognised him, they sent word throughout the
region and brought all who were sick to him, 36and
begged him that they might touch even the fringe
of his cloak; and all who touched it were healed.

chapter **FIFTEEN**

The **Tradition of the Elders**

Then Pharisees and scribes came to Jesus from
Jerusalem and said, 2'Why do your disciples
break the tradition of the elders? For they do not
wash their hands before they eat.' 3He answered
them, 'And why do you break the commandment
of God for the sake of your tradition? 4For God
said, "Honour your father and your mother," and,
"Whoever speaks evil of father or mother must
surely die." 5But you say that whoever tells father
or mother, "Whatever support you might have had
from me is given to God", then that person need
not honour the father. 6So, for the sake of your
tradition, you make void the word of God. 7You
hypocrites! Isaiah prophesied rightly about you
when he said:
8"This people honours me with their lips,
but their hearts are far from me;
9in vain do they worship me,
teaching human precepts as doctrines."'

James Tissot (French, 1836–1902) · The Pharisees and the Herodians Conspire Against Jesus (Les pharisiens et les hérodiens conspirent contre Jésus) · 1886–1894. *Opaque watercolor over graphite on gray wove paper, Image: 6 3/4 x 8 15/16 in. (17.1 x 22.7 cm). Brooklyn Museum, Purchased by public subscription, 00.159.97*

Things That **Defile**

10Then he called the crowd to him and said to
them, 'Listen and understand: 11it is not what goes
into the mouth that defiles a person, but it is
what comes out of the mouth that defiles.' 12Then
the disciples approached and said to him, 'Do
you know that the Pharisees took offence when
they heard what you said?' 13He answered, 'Every
plant that my heavenly Father has not planted
will be uprooted. 14Let them alone; they are blind
guides of the blind. And if one blind person guides
another, both will fall into a pit.' 15But Peter said
to him, 'Explain this parable to us.' 16Then he said,
'Are you also still without understanding? 17Do
you not see that whatever goes into the mouth
enters the stomach, and goes out into the sewer?
18But what comes out of the mouth proceeds
from the heart, and this is what defiles. 19For
out of the heart come evil intentions, murder,
adultery, fornication, theft, false witness, slander.
20These are what defile a person, but to eat with
unwashed hands does not defile.'

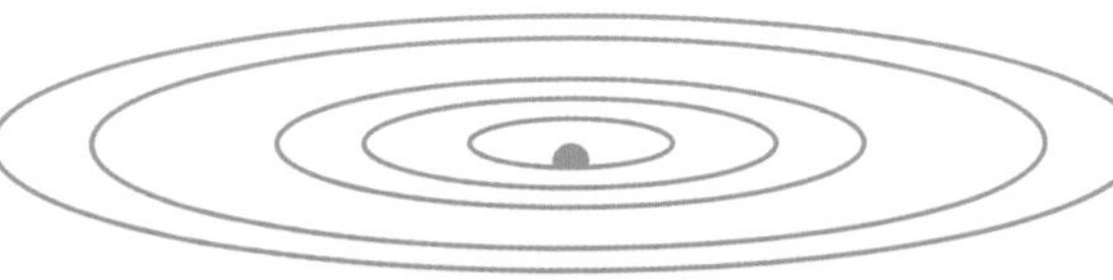

Jean Colombe · Christ and the Canaanite Woman · c. 1410

The Canaanite Woman's **Faith**

21 Jesus left that place and went away to the district of Tyre and Sidon. 22 Just then a Canaanite woman from that region came out and started shouting, 'Have mercy on me, Lord, Son of David; my daughter is tormented by a demon.' 23 But he did not answer her at all. And his disciples came and urged him, saying, 'Send her away, for she keeps shouting after us.' 24 He answered, 'I was sent only to the lost sheep of the house of Israel.' 25 But she came and knelt before him, saying, 'Lord, help me.' 26 He answered, 'It is not fair to take the children's food and throw it to the dogs.' 27 She said, 'Yes, Lord, yet even the dogs eat the crumbs that fall from their master's table.' 28 Then Jesus answered her, 'Woman, great is your faith! Let it be done for you as you wish.' And her daughter was healed instantly.

Jesus Cures Many People

29 After Jesus had left that place, he passed along the Sea of Galilee, and he went up the mountain, where he sat down. 30 Great crowds came to him, bringing with them the lame, the maimed, the blind, the mute, and many others. They put them at his feet, and he cured them, 31 so that the crowd was amazed when they saw the mute speaking, the maimed whole, the lame walking, and the blind seeing. And they praised the God of Israel.

James Tissot (French, 1836–1902) · Jesus Heals the Blind and Lame on the Mountain (Sur la montagne Jésus guérit les aveugles et les boiteux) · 1886–1896. *Opaque watercolor over graphite on gray wove paper, Image: 6 3/4 x 9 3/16 in. (17.1 x 23.3 cm). Brooklyn Museum, Purchased by public subscription, 00.159.88*

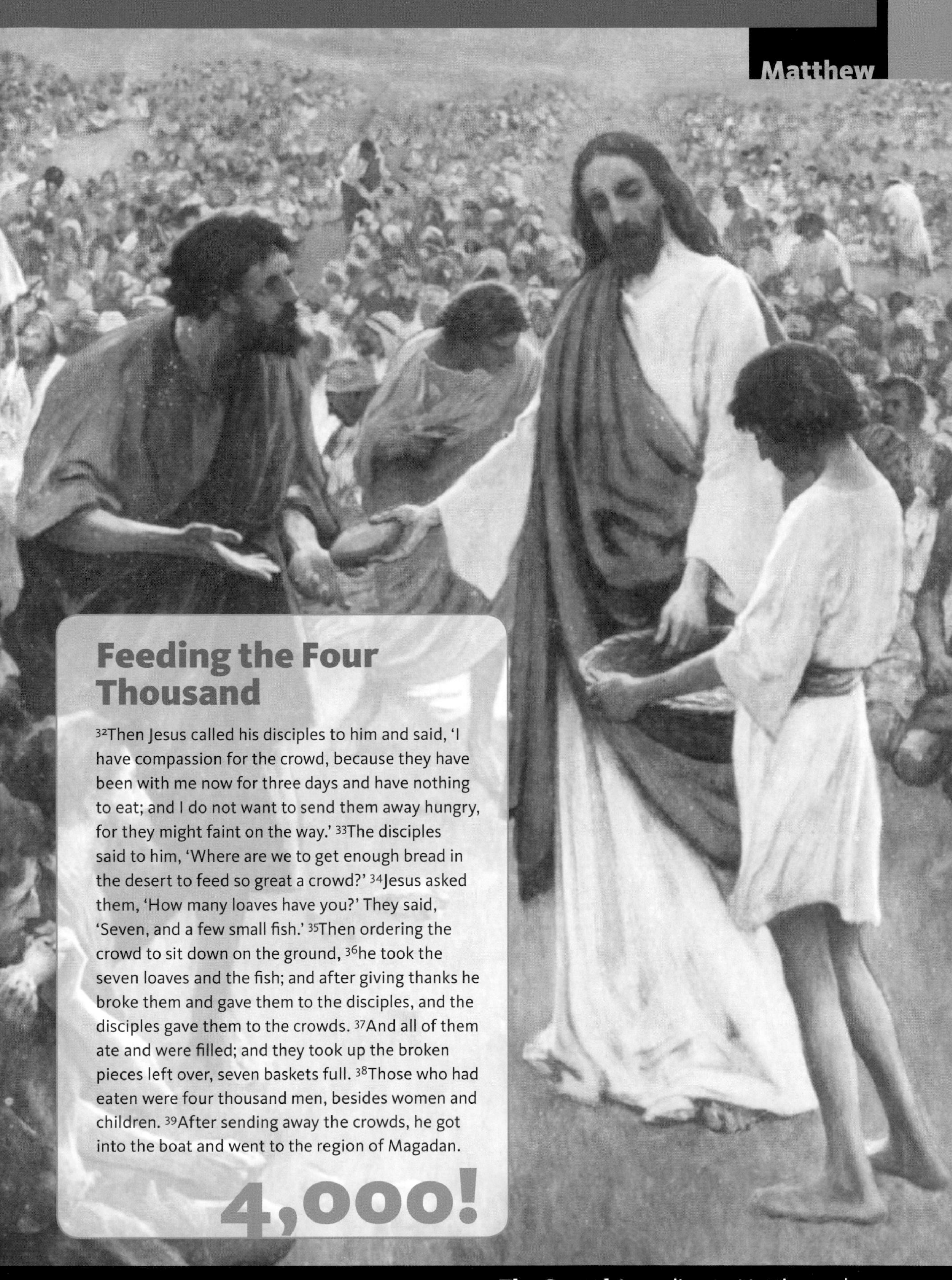

Feeding the Four Thousand

32Then Jesus called his disciples to him and said, 'I
have compassion for the crowd, because they have
been with me now for three days and have nothing
to eat; and I do not want to send them away hungry,
for they might faint on the way.' 33The disciples
said to him, 'Where are we to get enough bread in
the desert to feed so great a crowd?' 34Jesus asked
them, 'How many loaves have you?' They said,
'Seven, and a few small fish.' 35Then ordering the
crowd to sit down on the ground, 36he took the
seven loaves and the fish; and after giving thanks he
broke them and gave them to the disciples, and the
disciples gave them to the crowds. 37And all of them
ate and were filled; and they took up the broken
pieces left over, seven baskets full. 38Those who had
eaten were four thousand men, besides women and
children. 39After sending away the crowds, he got
into the boat and went to the region of Magadan.

4,000!

chapter **SIXTEEN**

The **Demand** for **a Sign**

The Pharisees and Sadducees came, and to test
Jesus they asked him to show them a sign from
heaven. 2He answered them, 'When it is evening,
you say, "It will be fair weather, for the sky is red."
3And in the morning, "It will be stormy today, for
the sky is red and threatening." You know how
to interpret the appearance of the sky, but you
cannot interpret the signs of the times. 4An evil
and adulterous generation asks for a sign, but no
sign will be given to it except the sign of Jonah.'
Then he left them and went away.

The Yeast of the **Pharisees** and **Sadducees**

5When the disciples reached the other side, they
had forgotten to bring any bread. 6Jesus said to
them, 'Watch out, and beware of the yeast of
the Pharisees and Sadducees.' 7They said to one
another, 'It is because we have brought no bread.'
8And becoming aware of it, Jesus said, 'You of
little faith, why are you talking about having no
bread? 9Do you still not perceive? Do you not
remember the five loaves for the five thousand,
and how many baskets you gathered? 10Or the
seven loaves for the four thousand, and how
many baskets you gathered? 11How could you
fail to perceive that I was not speaking about
bread? Beware of the yeast of the Pharisees and
Sadducees!' 12Then they understood that he had
not told them to beware of the yeast of bread, but
of the teaching of the Pharisees and Sadducees.

Peter's Declaration about Jesus

13Now when Jesus came into the district of
Caesarea Philippi, he asked his disciples, 'Who do
people say that the Son of Man is?' 14And they
said, 'Some say John the Baptist, but others Elijah,
and still others Jeremiah or one of the prophets.'
15He said to them, 'But who do you say that I am?'
16Simon Peter answered, 'You are the Messiah,
the Son of the living God.' 17And Jesus answered
him, 'Blessed are you, Simon son of Jonah! For
flesh and blood has not revealed this to you, but
my Father in heaven. 18And I tell you, you are
Peter, and on this rock I will build my church, and
the gates of Hades will not prevail against it. 19I
will give you the keys of the kingdom of heaven,

and whatever you bind on earth will be
bound in heaven, and whatever you loose
on earth will be loosed in heaven.' 20Then
he sternly ordered the disciples not to tell
anyone that he was the Messiah.

Jesus Foretells His Death and Resurrection

21From that time on, Jesus began to show
his disciples that he must go to Jerusalem
and undergo great suffering at the hands
of the elders and chief priests and scribes,
and be killed, and on the third day be
raised. 22And Peter took him aside and
began to rebuke him, saying, 'God forbid
it, Lord! This must never happen to you.'
23But he turned and said to Peter, 'Get
behind me, Satan! You are a stumbling-
block to me; for you are setting your mind
not on divine things but on human things.'

The Cross and Self-Denial

24Then Jesus told his disciples, 'If any want
to become my followers, let them deny
themselves and take up their cross and
follow me. 25For those who want to save
their life will lose it, and those who lose
their life for my sake will find it. 26For what
will it profit them if they gain the whole
world but forfeit their life? Or what will
they give in return for their life?

27'For the Son of Man is to come with his
angels in the glory of his Father, and then
he will repay everyone for what has been
done. 28Truly I tell you, there are some
standing here who will not taste death
before they see the Son of Man coming in
his kingdom.'

chapter SEVENTEEN

The Transfiguration

Six days later, Jesus took with him Peter and
James and his brother John and led them up
a high mountain, by themselves. [2]And he was
transfigured before them, and his face shone like
the sun, and his clothes became dazzling white.
[3]Suddenly there appeared to them Moses and
Elijah, talking with him. [4]Then Peter said to Jesus,
'Lord, it is good for us to be here; if you wish, I
will make three dwellings here, one for you, one
for Moses, and one for Elijah.' [5]While he was still
speaking, suddenly a bright cloud overshadowed
them, and from the cloud a voice said, 'This is
my Son, the Beloved; with him I am well pleased;
listen to him!' [6]When the disciples heard this, they
fell to the ground and were overcome by fear. [7]But
Jesus came and touched them, saying, 'Get up and
do not be afraid.' [8]And when they looked up, they
saw no one except Jesus himself alone.

9As they were coming down the mountain, Jesus
ordered them, 'Tell no one about the vision until
after the Son of Man has been raised from the
dead.' 10And the disciples asked him, 'Why, then,
do the scribes say that Elijah must come first?'
11He replied, 'Elijah is indeed coming and will
restore all things; 12but I tell you that Elijah has
already come, and they did not Recognise him,
but they did to him whatever they pleased. So also
the Son of Man is about to suffer at their hands.'
13Then the disciples understood that he was
speaking to them about John the Baptist.

Jesus Cures a Boy with a Demon

14When they came to the crowd, a man came
to him, knelt before him, 15and said, 'Lord, have
mercy on my son, for he is an epileptic and he
suffers terribly; he often falls into the fire and
often into the water. 16And I brought him to your
disciples, but they could not cure him.' 17Jesus
answered, 'You faithless and perverse generation,
how much longer must I be with you? How much
longer must I put up with you? Bring him here
to me.' 18And Jesus rebuked the demon, and it
came out of him, and the boy was cured instantly.
19Then the disciples came to Jesus privately and
said, 'Why could we not cast it out?' 20He said to
them, 'Because of your little faith. For truly I tell
you, if you have faith the size of a mustard seed,
you will say to this mountain, "Move from here
to there", and it will move; and nothing will be
impossible for you.'

Jesus Again **Foretells His Death** and **Resurrection**

22As they were gathering in Galilee, Jesus said to
them, 'The Son of Man is going to be betrayed into
human hands, 23and they will kill him, and on the
third day he will be raised.' And they were greatly
distressed.

Jesus and the **Temple Tax**

24When they reached Capernaum, the collectors of
the temple tax came to Peter and said, 'Does your
teacher not pay the temple tax?' 25He said, 'Yes,
he does.' And when he came home, Jesus spoke of
it first, asking, 'What do you think, Simon? From
whom do kings of the earth take toll or tribute?
From their children or from others?' 26When Peter
said, 'From others', Jesus said to him, 'Then the
children are free. 27However, so that we do not give
offence to them, go to the lake and cast a hook; take
the first fish that comes up; and when you open its
mouth, you will find a coin; take that and give it to
them for you and me.'

Follower of Marinus van Reymerswaele · The Misers· 1458–1463

Further **Teachings of** Jesus (18:1–20:34)

Jesus speaks of **community** and **forgiveness**.

chapter EIGHTEEN

True **Greatness**

At that time the disciples came to Jesus and asked, 'Who is the greatest in the kingdom of heaven?' 2He called a child, whom he put among them, 3and said, 'Truly I tell you, unless you change and become like children, you will never enter the kingdom of heaven. 4Whoever becomes humble like this child is the greatest in the kingdom of heaven. 5Whoever welcomes one such child in my name welcomes me.

Temptations to Sin

6'If any of you put a stumbling-block before one of these little ones who believe in me, it would be better for you if a great millstone were fastened around your neck and you were drowned in the depth of the sea. 7Woe to the world because of stumbling-blocks! Occasions for stumbling are bound to come, but woe to the one by whom the stumbling-block comes!

8'If your hand or your foot causes you to stumble, cut it off and throw it away; it is better for you to enter life maimed or lame than to have two hands or two feet and to be thrown into the eternal fire. 9And if your eye causes you to stumble, tear it out and throw it away; it is better for you to enter life with one eye than to have two eyes and to be thrown into the hell of fire.

The Parable of the **Lost Sheep**

10'Take care that you do not despise one of these little ones; for, I tell you, in heaven their angels continually see the face of my Father in heaven. 12What do you think? If a shepherd has a hundred sheep, and one of them has gone astray, does he not leave the ninety-nine on the mountains and go in search of the one that went astray? 13And if he finds it, truly I tell you, he rejoices over it more than over the ninety-nine that never went astray. 14So it is not the will of your Father in heaven that one of these little ones should be lost.

Reproving Another Who Sins

15'If another member of the church sins against you, go and point out the fault when the two of you are alone. If the member listens to you, you have regained that one. 16But if you are not listened to, take one or two others along with you, so that every word may be confirmed by the evidence of two or three witnesses. 17If the member refuses to listen to them, tell it to the church; and if the offender refuses to listen even to the church, let such a one be to you as a Gentile and a tax-collector. 18Truly I tell you, whatever you bind on earth will be bound in heaven, and whatever you loose on earth will be loosed in heaven. 19Again, truly I tell you, if two of you agree on earth about anything you ask, it will be done for you by my Father in heaven. 20For where two or three are gathered in my name, I am there among them.'

> 'Truly I tell you, unless you change and become like children, you will never enter the kingdom of heaven.'

Forgiveness

21 Then Peter came and said to him, 'Lord, if
another member of the church sins against me,
how often should I forgive? As many as seven
times?' 22 Jesus said to him, 'Not seven times, but, I
tell you, seventy-seven times.

The Parable of the **Unforgiving Servant**

23 'For this reason the kingdom of heaven may be
compared to a king who wished to settle accounts
with his slaves. 24 When he began the reckoning,
one who owed him ten thousand talents was
brought to him; 25 and, as he could not pay, his lord
ordered him to be sold, together with his wife and
children and all his possessions, and payment to be
made. 26 So the slave fell on his knees before him,
saying, "Have patience with me, and I will pay you
everything." 27 And out of pity for him, the lord of
that slave released him and forgave him the debt.
28 But that same slave, as he went out, came upon
one of his fellow-slaves who owed him a hundred
denarii; and seizing him by the throat, he said,
"Pay what you owe." 29 Then his fellow-slave fell
down and pleaded with him, "Have patience with
me, and I will pay you." 30 But he refused; then he
went and threw him into prison until he should pay
the debt. 31 When his fellow-slaves
saw what had happened, they were
greatly distressed, and they went
and reported to their lord all that
had taken place. 32 Then his lord
summoned him and said to him,
"You wicked slave! I forgave
you all that debt because you pleaded with me.
33 Should you not have had mercy on your fellow-
slave, as I had mercy on you?" 34 And in anger his
lord handed him over to be tortured until he should
pay his entire debt. 35 So my heavenly Father will
also do to every one of you, if you do not forgive
your brother or sister from your heart.'

chapter **NINETEEN**

Teaching about **Divorce**

When Jesus had finished saying these things,
he left Galilee and went to the region of Judea
beyond the Jordan. 2 Large crowds followed him,
and he cured them there.

3 Some Pharisees came to him, and to test him
they asked, 'Is it lawful for a man to divorce his
wife for any cause?' 4 He answered, 'Have you
not read that the one who made them at the
beginning "made them male and female", 5 and
said, "For this reason a man shall leave his father
and mother and be joined to his wife, and the
two shall become one flesh"? 6 So they are no
longer two, but one flesh. Therefore what God has
joined together, let no one separate.' 7 They said
to him, 'Why then did Moses command us to give
a certificate of dismissal and to divorce her?' 8 He
said to them, 'It was because you were so hard-
hearted that Moses allowed you to divorce your
wives, but at the beginning it was not so. 9 And
I say to you, whoever divorces his wife, except
for unchastity, and marries another commits
adultery.'

10His disciples said to him, 'If such is the case
of a man with his wife, it is better not to marry.'
11But he said to them, 'Not everyone can accept
this teaching, but only those to whom it is given.
12For there are eunuchs who have been so from
birth, and there are eunuchs who have been made
eunuchs by others, and there are eunuchs who
have made themselves eunuchs for the sake of the
kingdom of heaven. Let anyone accept this who
can.'

Jesus Blesses Little Children

13Then little children were being brought to him
in order that he might lay his hands on them and
pray. The disciples spoke sternly to those who
brought them; 14but Jesus said, 'Let the little
children come to me, and do not stop them; for
it is to such as these that the kingdom of heaven
belongs.' 15And he laid his hands on them and
went on his way.

The **Rich Young Man**

16Then someone came to him and said, 'Teacher,
what good deed must I do to have eternal
life?' 17And he said to him, 'Why do you ask me
about what is good? There is only one who is
good. If you wish to enter into life, keep the
commandments.' 18He said to him, 'Which ones?'
And Jesus said, 'You shall not murder; You shall
not commit adultery; You shall not steal; You shall
not bear false witness; 19Honour your father and
mother; also, You shall love your neighbour as
yourself.' 20The young man said to him, 'I have
kept all these; what do I still lack?' 21Jesus said
to him, 'If you wish to be perfect, go, sell your
possessions, and give the money to the poor,
and you will have treasure in heaven; then come,
follow me.' 22When the young man heard this
word, he went away grieving, for he had many
possessions.

23Then Jesus said to his disciples, 'Truly I tell
you, it will be hard for a rich person to enter the
kingdom of heaven. 24Again I tell you, it is easier
for a camel to go through the eye of a needle than
for someone who is rich to enter the kingdom of
God.' 25When the disciples heard this, they were
greatly astounded and said, 'Then who can be
saved?' 26But Jesus looked at them and said, 'For
mortals it is impossible, but for God all things are
possible.'

27Then Peter said in reply, 'Look, we have left
everything and followed you. What then will we
have?' 28Jesus said to them, 'Truly I tell you, at
the renewal of all things, when the Son of Man
is seated on the throne of his glory, you who
have followed me will also sit on twelve thrones,
judging the twelve tribes of Israel. 29And everyone
who has left houses or brothers or sisters or
father or mother or children or fields, for my
name's sake, will receive a hundredfold, and will
inherit eternal life. 30But many who are first will
be last, and the last will be first.

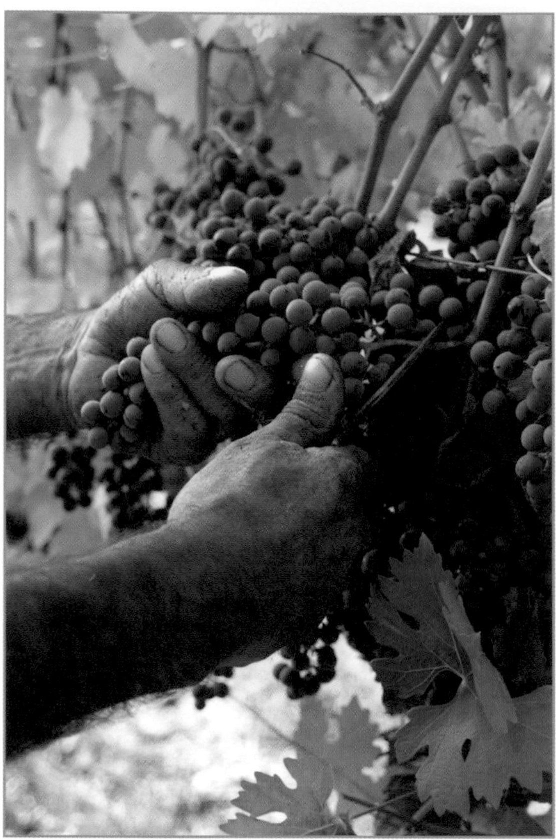

chapter **TWENTY**

The Labourers in the Vineyard

'For the kingdom of heaven is like a landowner
who went out early in the morning to hire
labourers for his vineyard. 2After agreeing with
the labourers for the usual daily wage, he sent
them into his vineyard. 3When he went out about
nine o'clock, he saw others standing idle in the
market-place; 4and he said to them, "You also go
into the vineyard, and I will pay you whatever is
right." So they went. 5When he went out again
about noon and about three o'clock, he did the
same. 6And about five o'clock he went out and
found others standing around; and he said to
them, "Why are you standing here idle all day?"
7They said to him, "Because no one has hired us."
He said to them, "You also go into the vineyard."
8When evening came, the owner of the vineyard
said to his manager, "Call the labourers and give
them their pay, beginning with the last and then
going to the first." 9When those hired about five
o'clock came, each of them received the usual
daily wage. 10Now when the first came, they
thought they would receive more; but each of
them also received the usual daily wage. 11And
when they received it, they grumbled against
the landowner, 12saying, "These last worked only
one hour, and you have made them equal to us
who have borne the burden of the day and the
scorching heat." 13But he replied to one of them,
"Friend, I am doing you no wrong; did you not
agree with me for the usual daily wage? 14Take
what belongs to you and go; I choose to give
to this last the same as I give to you. 15Am I not
allowed to do what I choose with what belongs to
me? Or are you envious because I am generous?"
16So the last will be first, and the first will be last.'

A Third Time Jesus Foretells His Death and Resurrection

17While Jesus was going up to Jerusalem, he took
the twelve disciples aside by themselves, and
said to them on the way, 18'See, we are going up
to Jerusalem, and the Son of Man will be handed
over to the chief priests and scribes, and they will
condemn him to death; 19then they will hand him
over to the Gentiles to be mocked and flogged
and crucified; and on the third day he will be
raised.'

The Request of the Mother of James and John

20 Then the mother of the sons of Zebedee came
to him with her sons, and kneeling before him, she
asked a favour of him. 21 And he said to her, 'What
do you want?' She said to him, 'Declare that these
two sons of mine will sit, one at your right hand
and one at your left, in your kingdom.' 22 But Jesus
answered, 'You do not know what you are asking.
Are you able to drink the cup that I am about to
drink?' They said to him, 'We are able.' 23 He said
to them, 'You will indeed drink my cup, but to sit
at my right hand and at my left, this is not mine
to grant, but it is for those for whom it has been
prepared by my Father.'

24 When the ten heard it, they were angry with the
two brothers. 25 But Jesus called them to him and
said, 'You know that the rulers of the Gentiles lord
it over them, and their great ones are tyrants over
them. 26 It will not be so among you; but whoever
wishes to be great among you must be your
servant, 27 and whoever wishes to be first among
you must be your slave; 28 just as the Son of Man
came not to be served but to serve, and to give his
life a ransom for many.'

Jesus Heals Two Blind Men

29 As they were leaving Jericho, a large crowd
followed him. 30 There were two blind men
sitting by the roadside. When they heard that
Jesus was passing by, they shouted, 'Lord, have
mercy on us, Son of David!' 31 The crowd sternly
ordered them to be quiet; but they shouted
even more loudly, 'Have mercy on us, Lord, Son
of David!' 32 Jesus stood still and called them,
saying, 'What do you want me to do for you?'
33 They said to him, 'Lord, let our eyes be opened.'
34 Moved with compassion, Jesus touched their
eyes. Immediately they regained their sight and
followed him.

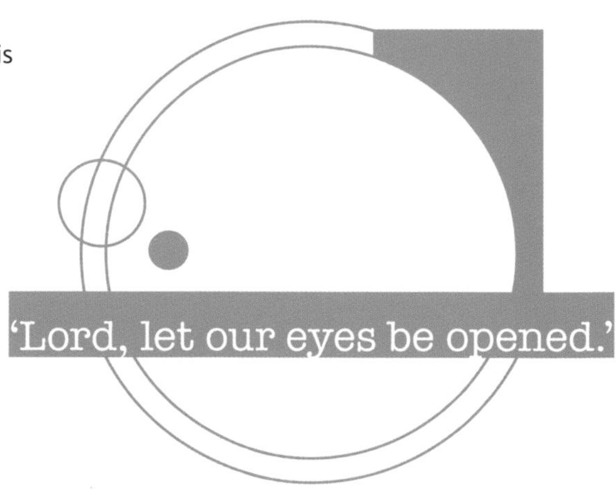
'Lord, let our eyes be opened.'

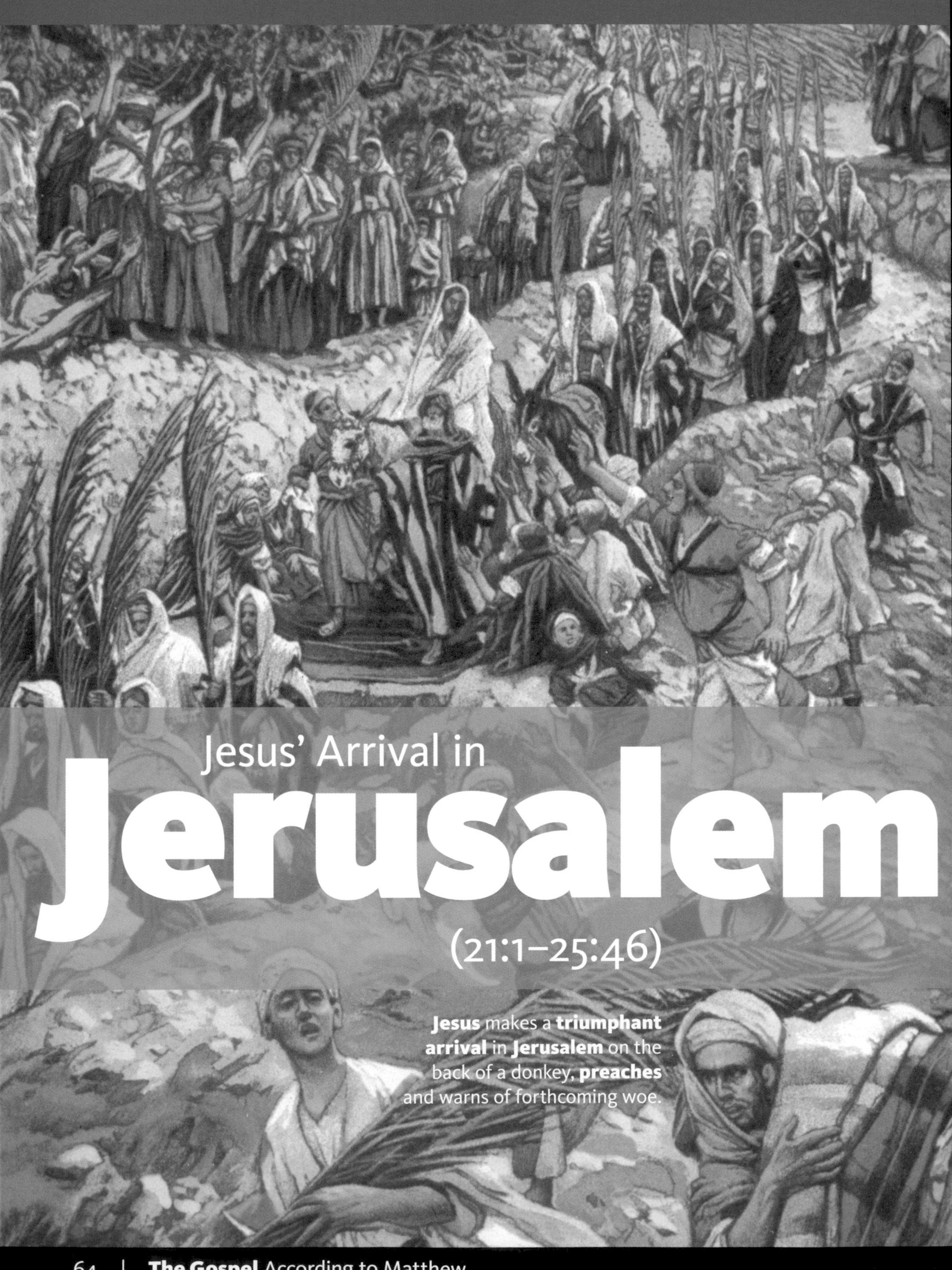

Jesus' Arrival in Jerusalem

(21:1–25:46)

Jesus makes a **triumphant arrival** in **Jerusalem** on the back of a donkey, **preaches** and warns of forthcoming woe.

chapter TWENTY-ONE

Jesus' **Triumphal Entry** into Jerusalem

When they had come near Jerusalem and had
reached Bethphage, at the Mount of Olives, Jesus
sent two disciples, 2saying to them, 'Go into the
village ahead of you, and immediately you will
find a donkey tied, and a colt with her; untie them
and bring them to me. 3If anyone says anything to
you, just say this, "The Lord needs them." And he
will send them immediately.' 4This took place to
fulfil what had been spoken through the prophet,
saying,
5'Tell the daughter of Zion,
Look, your king is coming to you,
humble, and mounted on a donkey,
and on a colt, the foal of a donkey.'
6The disciples went and did as Jesus had directed
them; 7they brought the donkey and the colt, and
put their cloaks on them, and he sat on them.
8A very large crowd spread their cloaks on the
road, and others cut branches from the trees and
spread them on the road. 9The crowds that went
ahead of him and that followed were shouting,
'Hosanna to the Son of David!
Blessed is the one who comes in the name of the
Lord!
Hosanna in the highest heaven!'
10When he entered Jerusalem, the whole city was
in turmoil, asking, 'Who is this?' 11The crowds were
saying, 'This is the prophet Jesus from Nazareth in
Galilee.'

Hosanna!

'Hosanna in the highest heaven!'

Jesus Cleanses the Temple

12Then Jesus entered the temple and drove out all
who were selling and buying in the temple, and he
overturned the tables of the money-changers and
the seats of those who sold doves. 13He said to
them, 'It is written,
"*My house shall be called a house of prayer*";
but you are making it a den of robbers.'

14 The blind and the lame came to him in the
temple, and he cured them. 15But when the chief
priests and the scribes saw the amazing things
that he did, and heard the children crying out in
the temple, 'Hosanna to the Son of David', they
became angry 16and said to him, 'Do you hear
what these are saying?' Jesus said to them, 'Yes;
have you never read,
"*Out of the mouths of infants and nursing babies
you have prepared praise for yourself*"?'
17He left them, went out of the city to Bethany,
and spent the night there.

Jesus Curses the Fig Tree

18In the morning, when he returned to the city, he
was hungry. 19And seeing a fig tree by the side of
the road, he went to it and found nothing at all on
it but leaves. Then he said to it, 'May no fruit ever
come from you again!' And the fig tree withered
at once. 20When the disciples saw it, they were
amazed, saying, 'How did the fig tree wither at
once?' 21Jesus answered them, 'Truly I tell you, if
you have faith and do not doubt, not only will you
do what has been done to the fig tree, but even if
you say to this mountain, "Be lifted up and thrown
into the sea", it will be done. 22Whatever you ask
for in prayer with faith, you will receive.'

The Authority of **Jesus Questioned**

23When he entered the temple, the chief priests
and the elders of the people came to him as he
was teaching, and said, 'By what authority are
you doing these things, and who gave you this
authority?' 24Jesus said to them, 'I will also ask you
one question; if you tell me the answer, then I will
also tell you by what authority I do these things.
25Did the baptism of John come from heaven, or
was it of human origin?' And they argued with
one another, 'If we say, "From heaven", he will say
to us, "Why then did you not believe him?" 26But
if we say, "Of human origin", we are afraid of the
crowd; for all regard John as a prophet.' 27So they
answered Jesus, 'We do not know.' And he said to
them, 'Neither will I tell you by what authority I
am doing these things.'

> ‘Whatever you ask for in prayer
> with faith, you will receive.’

The Parable of the **Two Sons**

28‘What do you think? A man had two sons; he
went to the first and said, “Son, go and work in
the vineyard today.” 29He answered, “I will not”;
but later he changed his mind and went. 30The
father went to the second and said the same; and
he answered, “I go, sir”; but he did not go. 31Which
of the two did the will of his father?’ They said,
‘The first.’ Jesus said to them, ‘Truly I tell you,
the tax-collectors and the prostitutes are going
into the kingdom of God ahead of you. 32For John
came to you in the way of righteousness and you
did not believe him, but the tax-collectors and the
prostitutes believed him; and even after you saw
it, you did not change your minds and believe him.

The Parable of the **Wicked Tenants**

33‘Listen to another parable. There was a
landowner who planted a vineyard, put a fence
around it, dug a wine press in it, and built a watch-
tower. Then he leased it to tenants and went to
another country. 34When the harvest time had
come, he sent his slaves to the tenants to collect
his produce. 35But the tenants seized his slaves
and beat one, killed another, and stoned another.
36Again he sent other slaves, more than the first;
and they treated them in the same way. 37Finally
he sent his son to them, saying, “They will respect
my son.” 38But when the tenants saw the son, they
said to themselves, “This is the heir; come, let us
kill him and get his inheritance.” 39So they seized
him, threw him out of the vineyard, and killed him.
40Now when the owner of the vineyard comes,
what will he do to those tenants?’ 41They said to
him, ‘He will put those wretches to a miserable
death, and lease the vineyard to other tenants who
will give him the produce at the harvest time.’
42Jesus said to them, ‘Have you never read in the
scriptures:
“*The stone that the builders rejected*
has become the cornerstone;
this was the Lord’s doing,
and it is amazing in our eyes”?
43Therefore I tell you, the kingdom of God will be
taken away from you and given to a people that
produces the fruits of the kingdom. 44The one
who falls on this stone will be broken to pieces;
and it will crush anyone on whom it falls.’
45When the chief priests and the Pharisees heard
his parables, they realised that he was speaking
about them. 46They wanted to arrest him, but
they feared the crowds, because they regarded
him as a prophet.

chapter **TWENTY-TWO**

The Parable of the **Wedding Banquet**

Once more Jesus spoke to them in parables,
saying: 2‘The kingdom of heaven may be
compared to a king who gave a wedding banquet
for his son. 3He sent his slaves to call those who
had been invited to the wedding banquet, but
they would not come. 4Again he sent other slaves,
saying, “Tell those who have been invited: Look,
I have prepared my dinner, my oxen and my fat
calves have been slaughtered, and everything is
ready; come to the wedding banquet.” 5But they
made light of it and went away, one to his farm,
another to his business, 6while the rest seized his
slaves, maltreated them, and killed them. 7The
king was enraged. He sent his troops, destroyed
those murderers, and burned their city. 8Then he
said to his slaves, “The wedding is ready, but those

> 'Give therefore to the emperor the things that are the emperor's, and to God the things that are God's.'

invited were not worthy. 9Go therefore into the
main streets, and invite everyone you find to the
wedding banquet." 10Those slaves went out into
the streets and gathered all whom they found,
both good and bad; so the wedding hall was filled
with guests.

11'But when the king came in to see the guests,
he noticed a man there who was not wearing a
wedding robe, 12and he said to him, "Friend, how
did you get in here without a wedding robe?" And
he was speechless. 13Then the king said to the
attendants, "Bind him hand and foot, and throw
him into the outer darkness, where there will be
weeping and gnashing of teeth." 14For many are
called, but few are chosen.'

The Question about **Paying Taxes**

15Then the Pharisees went and plotted to entrap
him in what he said. 16So they sent their disciples
to him, along with the Herodians, saying, 'Teacher,
we know that you are sincere, and teach the
way of God in accordance with truth, and show
deference to no one; for you do not regard people
with partiality. 17Tell us, then, what you think. Is it
lawful to pay taxes to the emperor, or not?' 18But
Jesus, aware of their malice, said, 'Why are you
putting me to the test, you hypocrites? 19Show me
the coin used for the tax.' And they brought him
a denarius. 20Then he said to them, 'Whose head
is this, and whose title?' 21They answered, 'The
emperor's.' Then he said to them, 'Give therefore
to the emperor the things that are the emperor's,
and to God the things that are God's.' 22When
they heard this, they were amazed; and they left
him and went away.

The Question about **the Resurrection**

23The same day some Sadducees came to him,
saying there is no resurrection; and they asked
him a question, saying, 24'Teacher, Moses said,
"If a man dies childless, his brother shall marry
the widow, and raise up children for his brother."
25Now there were seven brothers among us;
the first married, and died childless, leaving the
widow to his brother. 26The second did the same,
so also the third, down to the seventh. 27Last of
all, the woman herself died. 28In the resurrection,
then, whose wife of the seven will she be? For all
of them had married her.'

29Jesus answered them, 'You are wrong, because
you know neither the scriptures nor the power of

God. 30For in the resurrection they neither marry nor are given in marriage, but are like angels in heaven. 31And as for the resurrection of the dead, have you not read what was said to you by God, 32"I am the God of Abraham, the God of Isaac, and the God of Jacob"? He is God not of the dead, but of the living.' 33And when the crowd heard it, they were astounded at his teaching.

The Greatest Commandment

34When the Pharisees heard that he had silenced the Sadducees, they gathered together, 35and one of them, a lawyer, asked him a question to test him. 36'Teacher, which commandment in the law is the greatest?' 37He said to him, '"You shall love the Lord your God with all your heart, and with all your soul, and with all your mind." 38This is the greatest and first commandment. 39And a second is like it: "You shall love your neighbour as yourself." 40On these two commandments hang all the law and the prophets.'

The Question about **David's Son**

41Now while the Pharisees were gathered together, Jesus asked them this question: 42'What do you think of the Messiah? Whose son is he?' They said to him, 'The son of David.' 43He said to them, 'How is it then that David by the Spirit calls him Lord, saying,

44"The Lord said to my Lord,
'Sit at my right hand,
until I put your enemies under your feet'"?

45If David thus calls him Lord, how can he be his son?' 46No one was able to give him an answer, nor from that day did anyone dare to ask him any more questions.

chapter **TWENTY-THREE**

Jesus Denounces Scribes and Pharisees

Then Jesus said to the crowds and to his disciples, 2'The scribes and the Pharisees sit on Moses' seat; 3therefore, do whatever they teach you and follow it; but do not do as they do, for they do not practise what they teach. 4They tie up heavy burdens, hard to bear, and lay them on the shoulders of others; but they themselves are unwilling to lift a finger to move them. 5They do all their deeds to be seen by others; for they make their phylacteries broad and their fringes long. 6They love to have the place of honour at banquets and the best seats in the synagogues, 7and to be greeted with respect in the market-

places, and to have people call them rabbi. [8]But
you are not to be called rabbi, for you have
one teacher, and you are all students. [9]And call
no one your father on earth, for you have one
Father – the one in heaven. [10]Nor are you to be
called instructors, for you have one instructor,
the Messiah. [11]The greatest among you will be
your servant. [12]All who exalt themselves will be
humbled, and all who humble themselves will be
exalted.

[13]'But woe to you, scribes and Pharisees,
hypocrites! For you lock people out of the
kingdom of heaven. For you do not go in
yourselves, and when others are going in, you
stop them. [15]Woe to you, scribes and Pharisees,
hypocrites! For you cross sea and land to make
a single convert, and you make the new convert
twice as much a child of hell as yourselves.
[16]'Woe to you, blind guides, who say, "Whoever
swears by the sanctuary is bound by nothing, but
whoever swears by the gold of the sanctuary is
bound by the oath." [17]You blind fools! For which is
greater, the gold or the sanctuary that has made
the gold sacred? [18]And you say, "Whoever swears
by the altar is bound by nothing, but whoever
swears by the gift that is on the altar is bound
by the oath." [19]How blind you are! For which is
greater, the gift or the altar that makes the gift
sacred? [20]So whoever swears by the altar, swears
by it and by everything on it; [21]and whoever
swears by the sanctuary, swears by it and by the
one who dwells in it; [22]and whoever swears by
heaven, swears by the throne of God and by the
one who is seated upon it.

Woe!

[23]'Woe to you, scribes and Pharisees, hypocrites!
For you tithe mint, dill, and cummin, and have neglected the weightier matters of the law: justice and mercy and faith. It is these you ought to have practised without neglecting the others. [24]You
blind guides! You strain out a gnat but swallow a camel!
[25]'Woe to you, scribes and Pharisees, hypocrites!
For you clean the outside of the cup and of the plate, but inside they are full of greed and self-indulgence. [26]You blind Pharisee! First clean the
inside of the cup, so that the outside also may become clean.

[27]'Woe to you, scribes and Pharisees, hypocrites!
For you are like whitewashed tombs, which on the outside look beautiful, but inside they are full of the bones of the dead and of all kinds of filth. [28]So you also on the outside look righteous
to others, but inside you are full of hypocrisy and lawlessness.
[29]'Woe to you, scribes and Pharisees, hypocrites!
For you build the tombs of the prophets and decorate the graves of the righteous, [30]and
you say, "If we had lived in the days of our ancestors, we would not have taken part with them in shedding the blood of the prophets."
[31]Thus you testify against yourselves that you
are descendants of those who murdered the prophets. [32]Fill up, then, the measure of your
ancestors. [33]You snakes, you brood of vipers!
How can you escape being sentenced to hell?
[34]Therefore I send you prophets, sages, and
scribes, some of whom you will kill and crucify, and some you will flog in your synagogues and pursue from town to town, [35]so that upon you
may come all the righteous blood shed on earth, from the blood of righteous Abel to the blood of Zechariah son of Barachiah, whom you murdered between the sanctuary and the altar. [36]Truly I tell
you, all this will come upon this generation.

The **Lament** over Jerusalem

[37]'Jerusalem, Jerusalem, the city that kills the
prophets and stones those who are sent to it! How often have I desired to gather your children together as a hen gathers her brood under her wings, and you were not willing! [38]See, your house
is left to you, desolate. [39]For I tell you, you will
not see me again until you say, "Blessed is the one who comes in the name of the Lord."'

chapter **TWENTY-FOUR**

The **Destruction** of the **Temple** Foretold

As Jesus came out of the temple and was going
away, his disciples came to point out to him the
buildings of the temple. 2Then he asked them,
'You see all these, do you not? Truly I tell you, not
one stone will be left here upon another; all will
be thrown down.'

Signs of the **End of the Age**

3When he was sitting on the Mount of Olives,
the disciples came to him privately, saying, 'Tell
us, when will this be, and what will be the sign of
your coming and of the end of the age?' 4Jesus
answered them, 'Beware that no one leads you
astray. 5For many will come in my name, saying, "I
am the Messiah!" and they will lead many astray.
6And you will hear of wars and rumours of wars;
see that you are not alarmed; for this must take
place, but the end is not yet. 7For nation will rise
against nation, and kingdom against kingdom, and
there will be famines and earthquakes in various
places: 8all this is but the beginning of the birth
pangs.

Persecutions Foretold

9'Then they will hand you over to be tortured
and will put you to death, and you will be hated
by all nations because of my name. 10Then many
will fall away, and they will betray one another
and hate one another. 11And many false prophets
will arise and lead many astray. 12And because
of the increase of lawlessness, the love of many
will grow cold. 13But anyone who endures to the
end will be saved. 14And this good news of the
kingdom will be proclaimed throughout the world,
as a testimony to all the nations; and then the end
will come.

The Desolating **Sacrilege**

15'So when you see the desolating sacrilege
standing in the holy place, as was spoken of by
the prophet Daniel (let the reader understand),
16then those in Judea must flee to the mountains;
17someone on the housetop must not go down to
take what is in the house; 18someone in the field
must not turn back to get a coat. 19Woe to those

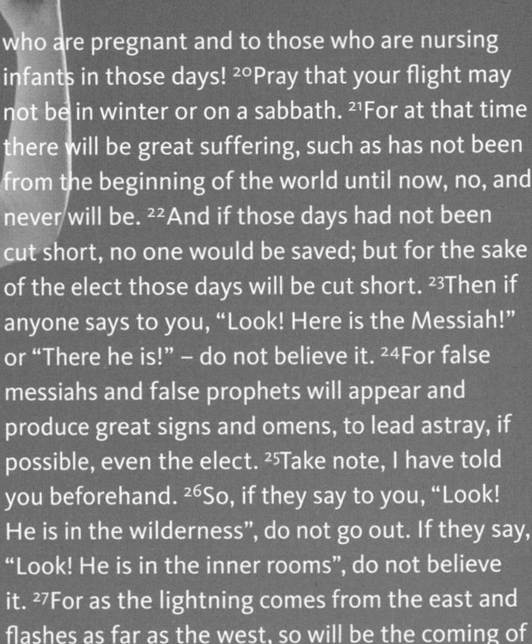

who are pregnant and to those who are nursing
infants in those days! 20Pray that your flight may
not be in winter or on a sabbath. 21For at that time
there will be great suffering, such as has not been
from the beginning of the world until now, no, and
never will be. 22And if those days had not been
cut short, no one would be saved; but for the sake
of the elect those days will be cut short. 23Then if
anyone says to you, "Look! Here is the Messiah!"
or "There he is!" – do not believe it. 24For false
messiahs and false prophets will appear and
produce great signs and omens, to lead astray, if
possible, even the elect. 25Take note, I have told
you beforehand. 26So, if they say to you, "Look!
He is in the wilderness", do not go out. If they say,
"Look! He is in the inner rooms", do not believe
it. 27For as the lightning comes from the east and
flashes as far as the west, so will be the coming of
the Son of Man. 28Wherever the corpse is, there
the vultures will gather.

The Coming of the **Son of Man**

29'Immediately after the suffering of those days
the sun will be darkened,
and the moon will not give its light;
the stars will fall from heaven,
and the powers of heaven will be shaken.
30Then the sign of the Son of Man will appear in
heaven, and then all the tribes of the earth will
mourn, and they will see "the Son of Man coming
on the clouds of heaven" with power and great
glory. 31And he will send out his angels with a loud
trumpet call, and they will gather his elect from the
four winds, from one end of heaven to the other.

Look!

' ... they will see "the Son of Man coming on the clouds of heaven".'

The Lesson of the **Fig Tree**

32‘From the fig tree learn its lesson: as soon as its branch becomes tender and puts forth its leaves, you know that summer is near. 33So also, when you see all these things, you know that he is near, at the very gates. 34Truly I tell you, this generation will not pass away until all these things have taken place. 35Heaven and earth will pass away, but my words will not pass away.

The Necessity for **Watchfulness**

36‘But about that day and hour no one knows, neither the angels of heaven, nor the Son, but only the Father. 37For as the days of Noah were, so will be the coming of the Son of Man. 38For as in those days before the flood they were eating and drinking, marrying and giving in marriage, until the day Noah entered the ark, 39and they knew nothing until the flood came and swept them all away, so too will be the coming of the Son of Man. 40Then two will be in the field; one will be taken and one will be left. 41Two women will be grinding meal together; one will be taken and one will be left. 42Keep awake therefore, for you do not know on what day your Lord is coming. 43But understand this: if the owner of the house had known in what part of the night the thief was coming, he would have stayed awake and would not have let his house be broken into. 44Therefore you also must be ready, for the Son of Man is coming at an unexpected hour.

The Faithful or the Unfaithful Slave

45‘Who then is the faithful and wise slave, whom his master has put in charge of his household, to give the other slaves their allowance of food at the proper time? 46Blessed is that slave whom his master will find at work when he arrives. 47Truly I tell you, he will put that one in charge of all his possessions. 48But if that wicked slave says to himself, “My master is delayed”, 49and he begins to beat his fellow-slaves, and eats and drinks with drunkards, 50the master of that slave will come on a day when he does not expect him and at an hour that he does not know. 51He will cut him in pieces and put him with the hypocrites, where there will be weeping and gnashing of teeth.

chapter TWENTY-FIVE

The Parable of the **Ten Bridesmaids**

‘Then the kingdom of heaven will be like this. Ten bridesmaids took their lamps and went to meet the bridegroom. 2Five of them were foolish, and five were wise. 3When the foolish took their lamps, they took no oil with them; 4but the wise took flasks of oil with their lamps. 5As the bridegroom was delayed, all of them became drowsy and slept. 6But at midnight there was a shout, “Look! Here is the bridegroom! Come out to meet him.” 7Then all those bridesmaids got up and trimmed their lamps. 8The foolish said to the wise, “Give us some of your oil, for our lamps are going out.” 9But the wise replied, “No! there will not be enough for you and for us; you had better go to the dealers and buy some for yourselves.” 10And while they went to buy it, the bridegroom

'Keep awake therefore, for you know
neither the day nor the hour.'

came, and those who were ready went with him
into the wedding banquet; and the door was
shut. [11]Later the other bridesmaids came also,
saying, "Lord, lord, open to us." [12]But he replied,
"Truly I tell you, I do not know you." [13]Keep awake
therefore, for you know neither the day nor the
hour.

The Parable of the **Talents**

[14]'For it is as if a man, going on a journey,
summoned his slaves and entrusted his property
to them; [15]to one he gave five talents, to another
two, to another one, to each according to his
ability. Then he went away. [16]The one who had
received the five talents went off at once and
traded with them, and made five more talents.
[17]In the same way, the one who had the two
talents made two more talents. [18]But the one
who had received the one talent went off and
dug a hole in the ground and hid his master's
money. [19]After a long time the master of those
slaves came and settled accounts with them.
[20]Then the one who had received the five talents
came forward, bringing five more talents, saying,
"Master, you handed over to me five talents; see,
I have made five more talents." [21]His master said
to him, "Well done, good and trustworthy slave;
you have been trustworthy in a few things, I will
put you in charge of many things; enter into the
joy of your master." [22]And the one with the two
talents also came forward, saying, "Master, you
handed over to me two talents; see, I have made
two more talents." [23]His master said to him, "Well
done, good and trustworthy slave; you have
been trustworthy in a few things, I will put you in
charge of many things; enter into the joy of your
master." [24]Then the one who had received the

one talent also came forward, saying, "Master, I
knew that you were a harsh man, reaping where
you did not sow, and gathering where you did not
scatter seed; 25so I was afraid, and I went and hid
your talent in the ground. Here you have what is
yours." 26But his master replied, "You wicked and
lazy slave! You knew, did you, that I reap where I
did not sow, and gather where I did not scatter?
27Then you ought to have invested my money
with the bankers, and on my return I would have
received what was my own with interest. 28So take
the talent from him, and give it to the one with
the ten talents. 29For to all those who have, more
will be given, and they will have an abundance;
but from those who have nothing, even what they
have will be taken away. 30As for this worthless
slave, throw him into the outer darkness, where
there will be weeping and gnashing of teeth."

The Judgement of the Nations

31'When the Son of Man comes in his glory, and all
the angels with him, then he will sit on the throne
of his glory. 32All the nations will be gathered
before him, and he will separate people one
from another as a shepherd separates the sheep
from the goats, 33and he will put the sheep at his
right hand and the goats at the left. 34Then the
king will say to those at his right hand, "Come,
you that are blessed by my Father, inherit the
kingdom prepared for you from the foundation
of the world; 35for I was hungry and you gave me
food, I was thirsty and you gave me something to
drink, I was a stranger and you welcomed me, 36I
was naked and you gave me clothing, I was sick
and you took care of me, I was in prison and you
visited me." 37Then the righteous will answer him,
"Lord, when was it that we saw you hungry and
gave you food, or thirsty and gave you something
to drink? 38And when was it that we saw you a
stranger and welcomed you, or naked and gave
you clothing? 39And when was it that we saw you
sick or in prison and visited you?" 40And the king
will answer them, "Truly I tell you, just as you did
it to one of the least of these who are members
of my family, you did it to me." 41Then he will say
to those at his left hand, "You that are accursed,
depart from me into the eternal fire prepared
for the devil and his angels; 42for I was hungry
and you gave me no food, I was thirsty and you
gave me nothing to drink, 43I was a stranger and
you did not welcome me, naked and you did not
give me clothing, sick and in prison and you did
not visit me." 44Then they also will answer, "Lord,
when was it that we saw you hungry or thirsty or
a stranger or naked or sick or in prison, and did
not take care of you?" 45Then he will answer them,
"Truly I tell you, just as you did not do it to one of
the least of these, you did not do it to me." 46And
these will go away into eternal punishment, but
the righteous into eternal life.'

'When the Son of Man comes in his glory, and all the angels with him, then he will sit on the throne of his glory.'

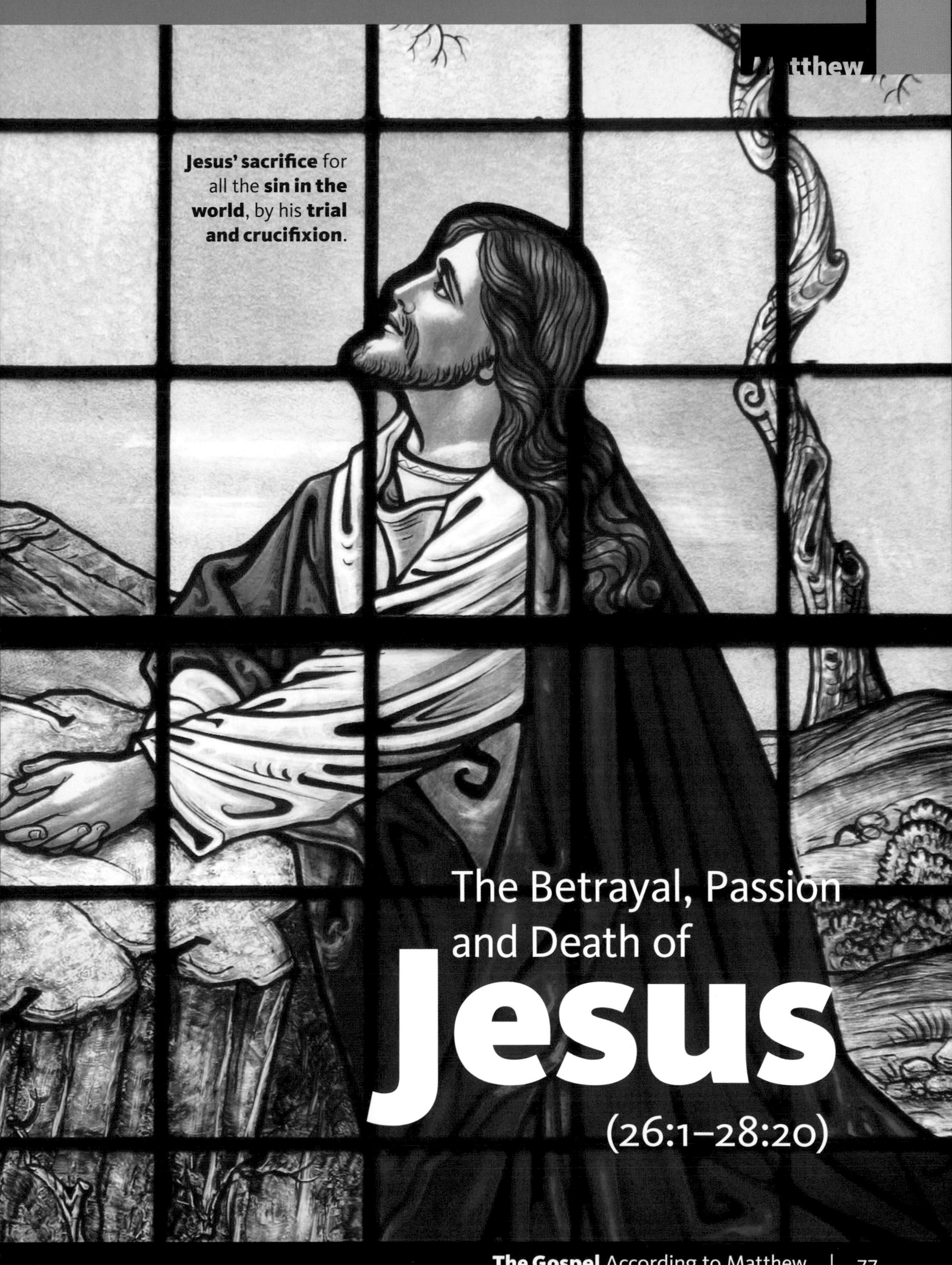

Jesus' sacrifice for all the **sin in the world**, by his **trial and crucifixion**.

The Betrayal, Passion and Death of Jesus (26:1–28:20)

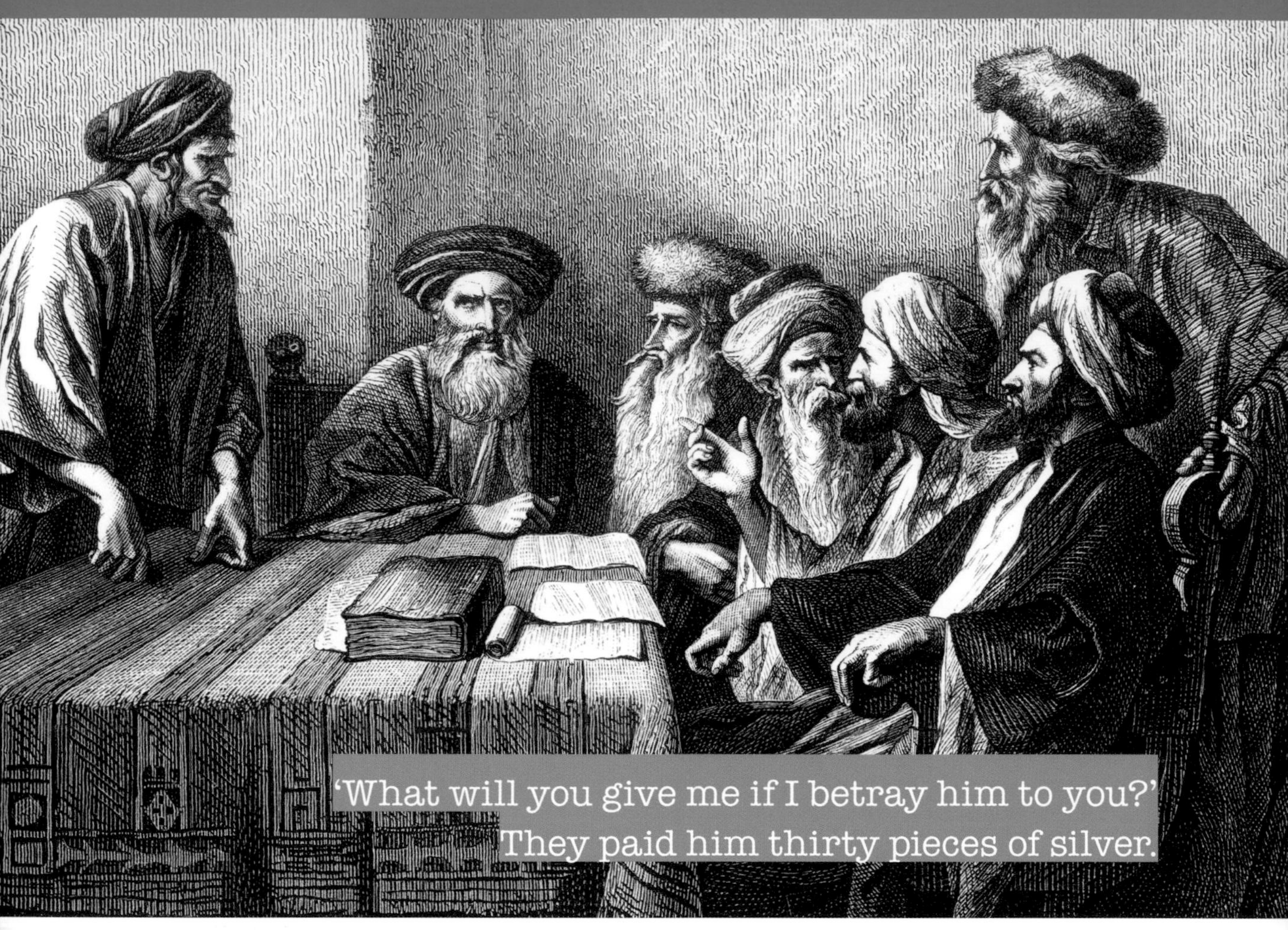
'What will you give me if I betray him to you?'
They paid him thirty pieces of silver.

chapter **TWENTY-SIX**

The Plot to Kill Jesus

When Jesus had finished saying all these things,
he said to his disciples, 2'You know that after two
days the Passover is coming, and the Son of Man
will be handed over to be crucified.'

3Then the chief priests and the elders of the
people gathered in the palace of the high priest,
who was called Caiaphas, 4and they conspired to
arrest Jesus by stealth and kill him. 5But they said,
'Not during the festival, or there may be a riot
among the people.'

The **Anointing** at Bethany

6Now while Jesus was at Bethany in the house
of Simon the leper, 7a woman came to him with
an alabaster jar of very costly ointment, and she
poured it on his head as he sat at the table. 8But
when the disciples saw it, they were angry and
said, 'Why this waste? 9For this ointment could
have been sold for a large sum, and the money
given to the poor.' 10But Jesus, aware of this, said
to them, 'Why do you trouble the woman? She
has performed a good service for me. 11For you
always have the poor with you, but you will not
always have me. 12By pouring this ointment on
my body she has prepared me for burial. 13Truly I
tell you, wherever this good news is proclaimed in
the whole world, what she has done will be told in
remembrance of her.'

Judas Agrees to **Betray** Jesus

14 Then one of the twelve, who was called Judas
Iscariot, went to the chief priests 15 and said, 'What
will you give me if I betray him to you?' They
paid him thirty pieces of silver. 16 And from that
moment he began to look for an opportunity to
betray him.

The Passover with the Disciples

17 On the first day of Unleavened Bread the
disciples came to Jesus, saying, 'Where do you
want us to make the preparations for you to eat
the Passover?' 18 He said, 'Go into the city to a
certain man, and say to him, "The Teacher says,
My time is near; I will keep the Passover at your
house with my disciples."' 19 So the disciples did as
Jesus had directed them, and they prepared the
Passover meal.

20 When it was evening, he took his place with
the twelve; 21 and while they were eating, he said,
'Truly I tell you, one of you will betray me.' 22 And
they became greatly distressed and began to say
to him one after another, 'Surely not I, Lord?' 23 He
answered, 'The one who has dipped his hand into
the bowl with me will betray me. 24 The Son of
Man goes as it is written of him, but woe to that
one by whom the Son of Man is betrayed! It would
have been better for that one not to have been
born.' 25 Judas, who betrayed him, said, 'Surely not
I, Rabbi?' He replied, 'You have said so.'

'Drink from it, all of you; for this is my blood of the covenant ...'

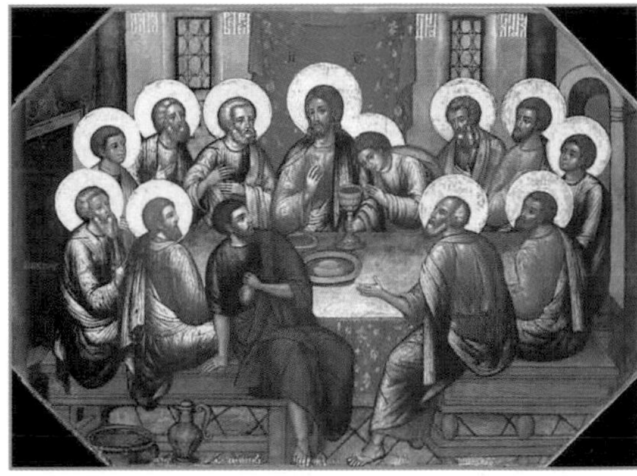

Simon Ushakov · The Last Supper · 1685

The Institution of the **Lord's Supper**

26 While they were eating, Jesus took a loaf of
bread, and after blessing it he broke it, gave it to
the disciples, and said, 'Take, eat; this is my body.'
27 Then he took a cup, and after giving thanks he
gave it to them, saying, 'Drink from it, all of you;
28 for this is my blood of the covenant, which is
poured out for many for the forgiveness of sins.
29 I tell you, I will never again drink of this fruit of
the vine until that day when I drink it new with
you in my Father's kingdom.'

30 When they had sung the hymn, they went out to
the Mount of Olives.

Peter's Denial Foretold

31 Then Jesus said to them, 'You will all become
deserters because of me this night; for it is
written,
"*I will strike the shepherd,*
and the sheep of the flock will be scattered."
32 But after I am raised up, I will go ahead of you to
Galilee.' 33 Peter said to him, 'Though all become
deserters because of you, I will never desert you.'

34Jesus said to him, 'Truly I tell you, this very night,
before the cock crows, you will deny me three
times.' 35Peter said to him, 'Even though I must die
with you, I will not deny you.' And so said all the
disciples.

Jesus Prays in **Gethsemane**

36Then Jesus went with them to a place called
Gethsemane; and he said to his disciples, 'Sit here
while I go over there and pray.' 37He took with him
Peter and the two sons of Zebedee, and began
to be grieved and agitated. 38Then he said to
them, 'I am deeply grieved, even to death; remain
here, and stay awake with me.' 39And going a
little farther, he threw himself on the ground and
prayed, 'My Father, if it is possible, let this cup
pass from me; yet not what I want but what you
want.' 40Then he came to the disciples and found
them sleeping; and he said to Peter, 'So, could you

not stay awake with me one hour? 41Stay awake
and pray that you may not come into the time of
trial; the spirit indeed is willing, but the flesh is
weak.' 42Again he went away for the second time
and prayed, 'My Father, if this cannot pass unless
I drink it, your will be done.' 43Again he came
and found them sleeping, for their eyes were
heavy. 44So leaving them again, he went away
and prayed for the third time, saying the same
words. 45Then he came to the disciples and said to
them, 'Are you still sleeping and taking your rest?
See, the hour is at hand, and the Son of Man is
betrayed into the hands of sinners. 46Get up, let
us be going. See, my betrayer is at hand.'

The Betrayal and Arrest of Jesus

47While he was still speaking, Judas, one of the
twelve, arrived; with him was a large crowd with
swords and clubs, from the chief priests and the
elders of the people. 48Now the betrayer had
given them a sign, saying, 'The one I will kiss is
the man; arrest him.' 49At once he came up to
Jesus and said, 'Greetings, Rabbi!' and kissed
him. 50Jesus said to him, 'Friend, do what you are
here to do.' Then they came and laid hands on
Jesus and arrested him. 51Suddenly, one of those
with Jesus put his hand on his sword, drew it, and
struck the slave of the high priest, cutting off
his ear. 52Then Jesus said to him, 'Put your sword
back into its place; for all who take the sword will
perish by the sword. 53Do you think that I cannot
appeal to my Father, and he will at once send me
more than twelve legions of angels? 54But how
then would the scriptures be fulfilled, which say it
must happen in this way?' 55At that hour Jesus said
to the crowds, 'Have you come out with swords
and clubs to arrest me as though I were a bandit?
Day after day I sat in the temple teaching, and you
did not arrest me. 56But all this has taken place,
so that the scriptures of the prophets may be
fulfilled.' Then all the disciples deserted him and
fled.

> 'So, could you not stay awake with me one hour? ... the spirit is willing, but the flesh is weak.'

Jesus Before the **High Priest**

57Those who had arrested Jesus took him to
Caiaphas the high priest, in whose house the
scribes and the elders had gathered. 58But Peter
was following him at a distance, as far as the
courtyard of the high priest; and going inside, he
sat with the guards in order to see how this would
end. 59Now the chief priests and the whole council
were looking for false testimony against Jesus so
that they might put him to death, 60but they found
none, though many false witnesses came forward.
At last two came forward 61and said, 'This fellow
said, "I am able to destroy the temple of God and
to build it in three days."' 62The high priest stood
up and said, 'Have you no answer? What is it that
they testify against you?' 63But Jesus was silent.
Then the high priest said to him, 'I put you under
oath before the living God, tell us if you are the
Messiah, the Son of God.' 64Jesus said to him, 'You
have said so. But I tell you,

From now on you will see the Son of Man
 seated at the right hand of Power
 and coming on the clouds of heaven.'

65Then the high priest tore his clothes and said, 'He
has blasphemed! Why do we still need witnesses?
You have now heard his blasphemy. 66What is your
verdict?' They answered, 'He deserves death.'
67Then they spat in his face and struck him; and
some slapped him, 68saying, 'Prophesy to us, you
Messiah! Who is it that struck you?'

Peter's Denial of Jesus

69Now Peter was sitting outside in the courtyard.
A servant-girl came to him and said, 'You also
were with Jesus the Galilean.' 70But he denied it
before all of them, saying, 'I do not know what
you are talking about.' 71When he went out to
the porch, another servant-girl saw him, and she
said to the bystanders, 'This man was with Jesus
of Nazareth.' 72Again he denied it with an oath,
'I do not know the man.' 73After a little while the
bystanders came up and said to Peter, 'Certainly
you are also one of them, for your accent betrays
you.' 74Then he began to curse, and he swore an
oath, 'I do not know the man!' At that moment
the cock crowed. 75Then Peter remembered what
Jesus had said: 'Before the cock crows, you will
deny me three times.' And he went out and wept
bitterly.

chapter TWENTY-SEVEN

Jesus Brought Before Pilate

When morning came, all the chief priests and the
elders of the people conferred together against
Jesus in order to bring about his death. 2They
bound him, led him away, and handed him over to
Pilate the governor.

The Suicide of Judas

3When Judas, his betrayer, saw that Jesus was
condemned, he repented and brought back the
thirty pieces of silver to the chief priests and
the elders. 4He said, 'I have sinned by betraying
innocent blood.' But they said, 'What is that to us?
See to it yourself.' 5Throwing down the pieces of

silver in the temple, he departed; and he went and
hanged himself. 6But the chief priests, taking the
pieces of silver, said, 'It is not lawful to put them
into the treasury, since they are blood money.'
7After conferring together, they used them to buy
the potter's field as a place to bury foreigners.
8For this reason that field has been called the
Field of Blood to this day. 9Then was fulfilled what
had been spoken through the prophet Jeremiah,
'And they took the thirty pieces of silver, the
price of the one on whom a price had been set, on
whom some of the people of Israel had set a price,
10and they gave them for the potter's field, as the
Lord commanded me.'

Pilate **Questions** Jesus

11Now Jesus stood before the governor; and the
governor asked him, 'Are you the King of the
Jews?' Jesus said, 'You say so.' 12But when he was
accused by the chief priests and elders, he did not
answer. 13Then Pilate said to him, 'Do you not hear
how many accusations they make against you?'
14But he gave him no answer, not even to a single
charge, so that the governor was greatly amazed.

Barabbas or **Jesus**?

15Now at the festival the governor was accustomed
to release a prisoner for the crowd, anyone whom
they wanted. 16At that time they had a notorious
prisoner, called Jesus Barabbas. 17So after they had
gathered, Pilate said to them, 'Whom do you want
me to release for you, Jesus Barabbas or Jesus who
is called the Messiah?' 18For he realised that it was
out of jealousy that they had handed him over.
19While he was sitting on the judgement seat, his
wife sent word to him, 'Have nothing to do with
that innocent man, for today I have suffered a
great deal because of a dream about him.' 20Now
the chief priests and the elders persuaded the
crowds to ask for Barabbas and to have Jesus
killed. 21The governor again said to them, 'Which
of the two do you want me to release for you?'
And they said, 'Barabbas.' 22Pilate said to them,
'Then what should I do with Jesus who is called the
Messiah?' All of them said, 'Let him be crucified!'
23Then he asked, 'Why, what evil has he done?' But
they shouted all the more, 'Let him be crucified!'

Pilate Hands Jesus over to be **Crucified**

24So when Pilate saw that he could do nothing,
but rather that a riot was beginning, he took
some water and washed his hands before the
crowd, saying, 'I am innocent of this man's blood;
see to it yourselves.' 25Then the people as a
whole answered, 'His blood be on us and on our
children!' 26So he released Barabbas for them; and
after flogging Jesus, he handed him over to be
crucified.

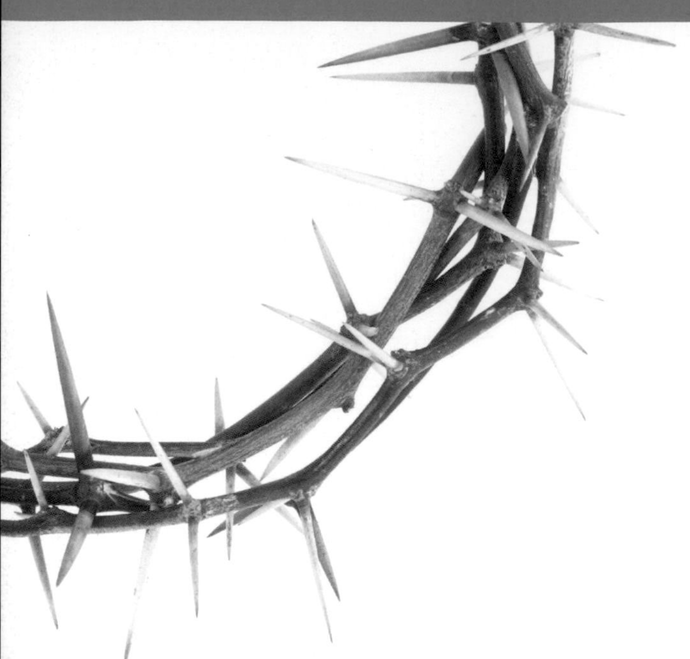

The Soldiers **Mock Jesus**

27 Then the soldiers of the governor took Jesus
into the governor's headquarters, and they
gathered the whole cohort around him. 28 They
stripped him and put a scarlet robe on him, 29 and
after twisting some thorns into a crown, they put
it on his head. They put a reed in his right hand
and knelt before him and mocked him, saying,
'Hail, King of the Jews!' 30 They spat on him, and
took the reed and struck him on the head. 31 After
mocking him, they stripped him of the robe and
put his own clothes on him. Then they led him
away to crucify him.

The Crucifixion of Jesus

32 As they went out, they came upon a man from
Cyrene named Simon; they compelled this man to
carry his cross. 33 And when they came to a place
called Golgotha (which means Place of a Skull),
34 they offered him wine to drink, mixed with gall;
but when he tasted it, he would not drink it. 35 And
when they had crucified him, they divided his
clothes among themselves by casting lots; 36 then

they sat down there and kept watch over him.
37 Over his head they put the charge against him,
which read, 'This is Jesus, the King of the Jews.'

38 Then two bandits were crucified with him, one
on his right and one on his left. 39 Those who
passed by derided him, shaking their heads 40 and
saying, 'You who would destroy the temple and
build it in three days, save yourself! If you are the
Son of God, come down from the cross.' 41 In the
same way the chief priests also, along with the
scribes and elders, were mocking him, saying,
42 'He saved others; he cannot save himself. He
is the King of Israel; let him come down from the
cross now, and we will believe in him. 43 He trusts
in God; let God deliver him now, if he wants to;
for he said, "I am God's Son."' 44 The bandits who
were crucified with him also taunted him in the
same way.

INRI

Sandro Botticelli · Lamentation of Christ · c. 1490

The Death of Jesus

45From noon on, darkness came over the whole
land until three in the afternoon. 46And about
three o'clock Jesus cried with a loud voice, 'Eli,
Eli, lema sabachthani?' that is, 'My God, my God,
why have you forsaken me?' 47When some of
the bystanders heard it, they said, 'This man is
calling for Elijah.' 48At once one of them ran and
got a sponge, filled it with sour wine, put it on a
stick, and gave it to him to drink. 49But the others
said, 'Wait, let us see whether Elijah will come to
save him.' 50Then Jesus cried again with a loud
voice and breathed his last. 51At that moment the
curtain of the temple was torn in two, from top
to bottom. The earth shook, and the rocks were
split. 52The tombs also were opened, and many
bodies of the saints who had fallen asleep were
raised. 53After his resurrection they came out of
the tombs and entered the holy city and appeared
to many. 54Now when the centurion and those
with him, who were keeping watch over Jesus, saw
the earthquake and what took place, they were
terrified and said, 'Truly this man was God's Son!'

55Many women were also there, looking on from a
distance; they had followed Jesus from Galilee and
had provided for him. 56Among them were Mary
Magdalene, and Mary the mother of James and
Joseph, and the mother of the sons of Zebedee.

The Burial of Jesus

57When it was evening, there came a rich man
from Arimathea, named Joseph, who was also a
disciple of Jesus. 58He went to Pilate and asked
for the body of Jesus; then Pilate ordered it to
be given to him. 59So Joseph took the body and

wrapped it in a clean linen cloth 60and laid it in his
own new tomb, which he had hewn in the rock. He
then rolled a great stone to the door of the tomb
and went away. 61Mary Magdalene and the other
Mary were there, sitting opposite the tomb.

The Guard **at the Tomb**

62The next day, that is, after the day of Preparation,
the chief priests and the Pharisees gathered
before Pilate 63and said, 'Sir, we remember what
that impostor said while he was still alive, "After
three days I will rise again." 64Therefore command
that the tomb be made secure until the third day;
otherwise his disciples may go and steal him away,
and tell the people, "He has been raised from the
dead", and the last deception would be worse than
the first.' 65Pilate said to them, 'You have a guard
of soldiers; go, make it as secure as you can.' 66So
they went with the guard and made the tomb
secure by sealing the stone.

chapter TWENTY-EIGHT

The Resurrection of Jesus

After the sabbath, as the first day of the week was dawning, Mary Magdalene and the other Mary went to see the tomb. 2And suddenly there was a great earthquake; for an angel of the Lord, descending from heaven, came and rolled back the stone and sat on it. 3His appearance was like lightning, and his clothing white as snow. 4For fear of him the guards shook and became like dead men. 5But the angel said to the women, 'Do not be afraid; I know that you are looking for Jesus who was crucified. 6He is not here; for he has been raised, as he said. Come, see the place where he lay. 7Then go quickly and tell his disciples, "He has been raised from the dead, and indeed he is going ahead of you to Galilee; there you will see him." This is my message for you.' 8So they left the tomb quickly with fear and great joy, and ran to tell his disciples. 9Suddenly Jesus met them and said, 'Greetings!' And they came to him, took hold of his feet, and worshipped him. 10Then Jesus said to them, 'Do not be afraid; go and tell my brothers to go to Galilee; there they will see me.'

The Report of the Guard

11While they were going, some of the guard went into the city and told the chief priests everything that had happened. 12After the priests had assembled with the elders, they devised a plan to give a large sum of money to the soldiers, 13telling them, 'You must say, "His disciples came by night and stole him away while we were asleep." 14If this comes to the governor's ears, we will satisfy him and keep you out of trouble.' 15So they took the money and did as they were directed. And this story is still told among the Jews to this day.

The **Commissioning** of the Disciples

16Now the eleven disciples went to Galilee, to the mountain to which Jesus had directed them. 17When they saw him, they worshipped him; but some doubted. 18And Jesus came and said to them, 'All authority in heaven and on earth has been given to me. 19Go therefore and make disciples of all nations, baptising them in the name of the Father and of the Son and of the Holy Spirit, 20and teaching them to obey everything that I have commanded you. And remember, I am with you always, to the end of the age.'

> 'Do not be afraid; I know that you are looking for Jesus who was crucified.
>
> He is not here; for he has been raised ...'

‘And remember, I am with you
always, to the end of the age!’

SECVND
VMMA
LIBER
GENERA
TIONIS
ESV
CHR
STI
FILIO
AVID
INITIV
EVANGE
LII IESV
CHRIST
DV
MAR
GVM
SECVN
DVM
LVCAM
FVIT
IN DI
HERO
DIS RE
GIS
IN PRIN
CIPIO ER
AT VERB
VM ET VE
RBVM ER

Lectio divina

Lectio divina (meaning 'divine reading' or 'holy reading') is an ancient method of paying attention to God's Word in Scripture in order to achieve a fuller understanding of the message and thus be better able to take it to heart in daily life. It was first practiced in the early Christian monasteries. Pope Benedict XVI said: 'I would like in particular to recall and recommend the ancient tradition of *lectio divina*: the diligent reading of Sacred Scripture accompanied by prayer brings about that intimate dialogue in which the person reading hears God who is speaking, and, in praying, responds with trusting openness of heart.'

Lectio divina is a particularly simple approach to prayer. It can be used individually or in groups. Ideally, you should choose the same time each day for this exercise and in a place free of distraction so that a daily habit will be learned.

So, choose a text of Scripture, something fairly brief and engaging. Then:

Lectio (read): Slowly read the text, being alert for God's Word to your life; notice what stands out for you or seems significant.

Meditatio (meditate): Read the text again. Pause and talk to God about what you are hearing. Meditation is like talking to God.

Contemplatio (contemplate): Read again. Now listen to and receive what God may be saying to you. Contemplation is like listening to God.

Oratio (pray): Recognise and pray whatever may be the deep desire of your heart.

Then some traditions add:

Actio (action): What does this study and prayer time call you to do? How will you take it to heart in your life now?

People from all walks of life are realising the benefits of this type of spiritual exercise. *Lectio divina* allows you to explore the deep wisdom of Scripture and to experience God in a very personal way.

Index

Chapter One
The Genealogy of Jesus the Messiah (1:1-17) 9
The Birth of Jesus the Messiah (1:18-25) 11

Chapter Two
The Visit of the Wise Men (2:1-12) 11
The Escape to Egypt (2:13-15) 12
The Massacre of the Infants (2:16-18) 12
The Return from Egypt (2:19-23) 12

Chapter Three
The Proclamation of John the Baptist (3:1-12) 13
The Baptism of Jesus (3:13-17) 14

Chapter Four
The Temptation of Jesus (4:1-11) 15
Jesus Begins His Ministry in Galilee (4:12-17) 15
Jesus Calls His First Disciples (4:18-22) 17
Jesus Ministers to Crowds of People (4:23-25) 17

Chapter Five
The Beatitudes (5:1-12) 18
Salt and Light (5:13-16) 18
The Law and the Prophets (5:17-20) 19
Concerning Anger (5:21-26) 19
Concerning Adultery (5:27-30) 19
Concerning Divorce (5:31-32) 20
Concerning Oaths (5:33-37) 20
Concerning Retaliation (5:38-42) 20
Love for Enemies (5:43-48) 21

Chapter Six
Concerning Almsgiving (6:1-4) 21
Concerning Prayer (6:5-15) 21
Concerning Fasting (6:16-18) 22
Concerning Treasures (6:19-21) 22
The Sound Eye (6:22-23) 22
Serving Two Masters (6:24) 22
Do Not Worry (6:25-34) 22

Chapter Seven
Judging Others (7:1-5) 23
Profaning the Holy (7:6) 23
Ask, Search, Knock (7:7-11) 23
The Golden Rule (7:12) 23
The Narrow Gate (7:13-14) 23
A Tree and its Fruit (7:15-20) 24
Concerning Self-Deception (7:21-23) 24
Hearers and Doers (7:24-29) 25

Chapter Eight
Jesus Cleanses a Leper (8:1-4) 26
Jesus Heals a Centurion's Servant (8:5-13) 27
Jesus Heals Many at Peter's House (8:14-17) 27
Would-Be Followers of Jesus (8:18-22) 27
Jesus Stills the Storm (8:23-27) 28
Jesus Heals the Gadarene Demoniacs (8:28-34) 28

Chapter Nine
Jesus Heals a Paralytic (9:1-8) 29
The Calling of Matthew (9:9-13) 29
The Question about Fasting (9:14-17) 30
A Girl Restored to Life and a Woman Healed (9:18-26) 30
Jesus Heals Two Blind Men (9:27-31) 30
Jesus Heals One Who Was Mute (9:32-34) 31
The Harvest is Great, the Labourers Few (9:35-38) 31

Chapter Ten
The Twelve Apostles (10:1-4) 33
The Mission of the Twelve (10:5-15) 33
Coming Persecutions (10:6-25) 34
Whom to Fear (10:26-33) 35
Not Peace, but a Sword (10:34-39) 35
Rewards (10:40-42) 35

Chapter Eleven
Messengers from John the Baptist (11:1-6) 36
Jesus Praises John the Baptist (11:7-19) 36
Woes to Unrepentant Cities (11:20-24) 37
Jesus Thanks His Father (11:25-30) 37

Chapter Twelve
Plucking Grain on the Sabbath (12:1-8) 37
The Man with the Withered Hand (12:9-14) 37
God's Chosen Servant (12:15-21) 38
Jesus and Beelzebul (12:22-32) 39
A Tree and Its Fruit (12:33-37) 39
The Sign of Jonah (12:38-42) 40
The Return of the Unclean Spirit (12:43-45) 40
The True Kindred of Jesus (12:46-50) 41

Chapter Thirteen
The Parable of the Sower (13:1-9) 43
The Purpose of the Parables (13:10-17) 43
The Parable of the Sower Explained (13:18-23) 44
The Parable of Weeds among the Wheat (13:24-30) 44
The Parable of the Mustard Seed (13:31-32) 45
The Parable of the Yeast (13:33) 45
The Use of Parables (13:34-35) 45
Jesus Explains the Parable of the Weeds (13:36-43) 45
Three Parables (13:44-50) 46
Treasures New and Old (13:51-53) 46
The Rejection of Jesus at Nazareth (13:54-58) 47

Chapter Fourteen
The Death of John the Baptist (14:1-12) 49
Feeding the Five Thousand (14:13-21) 49
Jesus Walks on Water (14:22-33) 50
Jesus Heals the Sick in Gennesaret (14:34-36) 51

Chapter Fifteen
The Tradition of the Elders (15:1-9) 51
Things That Defile (15:10-20) 51
The Canaanite Woman's Faith (15:21-28) 52
Jesus Cures Many People (15:29-31) 52
Feeding the Four Thousand (15:32-39) 53

Chapter Sixteen
The Demand for a Sign (16:1-4) 54
The Yeast of the Pharisees and Sadducees (16:5-12) 54
Peter's Declaration about Jesus (16:13-20) 54
Jesus Foretells His Death and Resurrection (16:21-23) 55
The Cross and Self-Denial (16:24-28) 55

Chapter Seventeen
The Transfiguration (17:1-13) 56
Jesus Cures a Boy with a Demon (17:14-21) 57
Jesus Again Foretells His Death and Resurrection (17:22-23) 57
Jesus and the Temple Tax (17:24-27) 57

Chapter Eighteen
True Greatness (18:1-5) 59
Temptations to Sin (18:6-9) 59
The Parable of the Lost Sheep (18:10-14) 59
Reproving Another Who Sins (18:15-20) 59
Forgiveness (18:21-22) 60
The Parable of the Unforgiving Servant (18:23-35) 60

Chapter Nineteen
Teaching about Divorce (19:1-12) 60
Jesus Blesses Little Children (19:13-15) 61
The Rich Young Man (19:16-30) 61

Chapter Twenty
The Labourers in the Vineyard (20:1-16) 62
A Third Time Jesus Foretells His Death and Resurrection (20:17-19) 62
The Request of the Mother of James and John (20:20-28) 63
Jesus Heals Two Blind Men (20:29-34) 63

Chapter Twenty-One
Jesus' Triumphal Entry into Jerusalem (21:1-11) 65
Jesus Cleanses the Temple (21:12-17) 65
Jesus Curses the Fig Tree (21:18-22) 66
The Authority of Jesus Questioned (21:23-27) 66
The Parable of the Two Sons (21:28-32) 67
The Parable of the Wicked Tenants (21:33-46) 67

Chapter Twenty-Two
The Parable of the Wedding Banquet (22:1-14) 67
The Question about Paying Taxes (22:15-22) 68
The Question about the Resurrection (22:23-33) 68
The Greatest Commandment (22:34-40) 69
The Question about David's Son (22:41-46) 69

Chapter Twenty-Three
Jesus Denounces Scribes and Pharisees (23:1-36) 69
The Lament over Jerusalem (23:37-39) 71

Chapter Twenty-Four
The Destruction of the Temple Foretold (24:1-2) 72
Signs of the End of the Age (24:3-8) 72
Persecutions Foretold (24:9-14) 72
The Desolating Sacrilege (24:15-28) 72
The Coming of the Son of Man (24:29-31) 73
The Lesson of the Fig Tree (24: 32-35) 74
The Necessity for Watchfulness (24:36-44) 74
The Faithful or the Unfaithful Slave (24:45-51) 74

Chapter Twenty-Five
The Parable of the Ten Bridesmaids (25:1-13) 74
The Parable of the Talents (25:14-30) 75
The Judgement of the Nations (25:31-46) 76

Chapter Twenty-Six
The Plot to Kill Jesus (26:1-5) 78
The Anointing at Bethany (26:6-13) 78
Judas Agrees to Betray Jesus (26:14-16) 79
The Passover with the Disciples (26:17-25) 79
The Institution of the Lord's Supper (26:26-30) 79
Peter's Denial Foretold (26:31-35) 79
Jesus Prays in Gethsemane (26:36-46) 80
The Betray and Arrest of Jesus (26:47-56) 81
Jesus Before the High Priest (26:57-68) 81
Peter's Denial of Jesus (26:69-75) 82

Chapter Twenty-Seven
Jesus Brought before Pilate (27:1-2) 82
The Suicide of Judas (27:3-10) 82
Pilate Questions Jesus (27:11-14) 83
Barabbas or Jesus? (27:15-23) 83
Pilate Hands Jesus over to be Crucified (27:24-26) 83
The Soldiers Mock Jesus (27:27-31) 84
The Crucifixion of Jesus (27:32-44) 84
The Death of Jesus (27:45-56) 86
The Burial of Jesus (27:57-61) 86
The Guard at the Tomb (27:62-66) 87

Chapter Twenty-Eight
The Resurrection of Jesus (28:1-10) 89
The Report of the Guard (28:11-15) 89
The Commissioning of the Disciples (28:16-20) 89